Gay Chicago Memories
1300 N. Wells

Owen Keehnen
Author of Man's Country: More Than a Bathhouse

RATTLING GOOD YARNS
PRESS

Rattling Good Yarns Press, LLC
33490 Date Palm Drive 3065
Cathedral City CA 92235
USA
www.rattlinggoodyarns.com

Cover Design: Rattling Good Yarns Press

Library of Congress Control Number: 2025939662
ISBN: 978-1-955826-93-8

First Edition

OWEN KEEHNEN

For Carl.
None of this would be possible without you

Contents

AUTHOR NOTE..I

FOREWORD II

INTRODUCTION IV

1355 N. WELLS 1

CAROL'S SPEAKEASY 10

BIJOU THEATER 104

THE GLORY HOLE..147

ARCADES: THE OVER 21 BOOKSTORE & THE PEEPING TOM 167

GAY CHICAGO 179

EPILOGUE..189

LOOKING BACK FROM THE END OF THE BLOCK......189

ACKNOWLEDGMENTS 190

ABOUT THE AUTHOR..191

Author Note

Gay Chicago Memories: 1300 N. Wells St. is a history culled from news accounts, columnist tidbits, and advertisements. However, the primary means of recreating this world resides in the over 100 interviews conducted with employees and patrons of the various gay businesses on the block. Memory can be a faulty storyteller, but as with much of history, the importance of the past resides in the role it played in people's lives. The 1300 block of North Wells played a big part in the individual and collective histories of Chicago's gay community. In the 1970s and 1980s, this stretch was a hub of LGBT social and sexual activity. It's all gone now, but sometimes memories offer a window onto a vanished world.

Foreword

In the days of sepia-toned photographs, when immigrants arrived in Chicago with battered suitcases, they settled in neighborhoods where their native tongue, traditions, and cuisine thrived. Chicago became a patchwork of vibrant communities—Polish, German, Greek—each with its distinctive heartbeat. Some of those neighborhoods remain today, but now they mostly stand as shadows, echoes of their storied pasts.

And we, the gay community, are no different. We've always sought out places of safety, drawn by the safety of numbers and the hope of belonging. Over the decades, Chicago has been home to several "safe-ish" enclaves of gay life: Towertown, Dearborn and Division, Clark and Diversey, and, of course, Lakeview. Some were cozy residential areas; others, commercial hubs where bars dotted the landscape like stars in the night. These places became our sanctuaries.

But post-Stonewall, one place stood out above all others: 1300 N. Wells St. Unlike the other gay areas, this stretch was electric, pulsing with a kind of raw energy and unfiltered freedom. Yes, it had the bars, but what really set it apart were the "sex venues" that lined the street—a magnet for those seeking not just a drink but a taste of liberation.

"It's time for liberation!" sang the Village People in 1980. And nowhere in Chicago did liberation bloom more boldly than on 1300 N. Wells St.

By the time I arrived in the Windy City in the early '90s, the golden age of 1300 N. Wells had already begun to fade. Only one bar, Carol's Speakeasy, remained from that era, and I visited it once before it too shuttered its doors.

I missed the wild, unbridled heyday of that iconic strip. But thanks to Owen Keehnen and his brilliant work gathering these vivid, unforgettable stories in Gay Chicago Memories: 1300 N. Wells St., I now know what I missed. And through these pages, I can imagine the freedom, the joy, and the fiery spirit of a time gone by.

—St Sukie de la Croix, 2025, Palm Springs, California

Introduction

When I moved to Chicago in 1984, I didn't have a car or a job. I arrived here from Quincy, Illinois, choosing Chicago because the train from Quincy went there. Shortly after arriving in my adopted town, I started job hunting. I found North Wells Street by chance.

I desperately wanted to work at the Ripley's Believe It or Not Museum at 1500 N. Wells St., but it wasn't in the cards. The museum was a bi-level "emporium of oddities" that opened on November 21, 1968. Some of the displays included the skull of a human unicorn, a two-headed calf, the world's largest hairball, the tiniest violin, and the largest pair of women's shoes—size 28! Also on display were Henry VIII's "gout shoes," the image of a man born with four eyes, a skull bowl, etc. My over-eagerness to work there was probably a red flag against my being hired.

After applying at several places that day, I was hired at Bizarre Bazaar (1517 N. Wells), an old hippie haunt turned urban drug store—literally. Bizarre Bazaar was an enormous single-room retail space with low ceilings, a cement floor, and a roll-up garage door entrance. Inside were three enormous sales stations with one employee in each area. The display case along the south wall had pipes, bongs, and assorted drug paraphernalia. I was stationed at the second retail area, an oval retail island that stretched the length of the store. My display case was a catchall filled with crystal figurines, punkish rings and pendants, beads, headbands, wristbands, sunglasses, Chicago souvenir items, as well as vintage cheesecake and beefcake playing cards. The third retail island featured wigs, hats, T-shirts, boas, greeting cards, etc.

The pay at Bizarre Bazaar was minimum wage plus commission, but the only station that made decent money was the drug paraphernalia case. I worked there for probably two weeks, but I spent my lunches exploring. On my first or second day on the job, I discovered the gritty stretch of 1300 North Wells—two peep shows, two gay bars, and the Bijou Theater. This was the sort of streetscape I had imagined when I fantasized about life in the big gay city.

The entire neighborhood was fascinating. In the late 1960s, Old Town was ground zero for the hippie and counterculture scene in Chicago. By then, the area had already been a haven for artists for almost 70 years. Old Town Triangle Association archivist, David Pfendler, cites the origin of the neighborhood's longtime artistic reputation, "The presence of artists in Old Town goes way back to the Columbian Exposition of 1893. The city felt that Chicago's cultural development wasn't as rapid as that of Boston and Philadelphia, so the powers that be encouraged Lambert Tree (1832-1910) to set up the Tree Studios near Michigan Avenue (4 E. Ohio), where artists who had been part of the World's Fair could live and have their studios.

"In the 1920s and '30s, the area became too expensive and artists came to Crilly Court (1700 N. Wells) because it reminded them of the Tree Studios. In the first 10 years of the Art Fair, at least 126 artists lived within our triangle area between Clark, North, and Ogden, and another 130 within a mile of the triangle." (Judy Carmack Bross, 'Old Town Art Fair: Treasures, Gardens, and Community Spirit.' *Classic Chicago Magazine.com*, June 4, 2017).

Postal worker Henry Gerber (1892-1972) resided at 1710 Crilly Court. It was there that Gerber founded the Society for Human Rights (SHR) on December 10, 1924. The short-lived group was granted a charter by the state of Illinois, becoming the first gay rights organization in the country. After only a few meetings, the Gerber residence was raided, arrests were made, papers were confiscated, and that was the end of the Society for Human Rights. During its short time in existence, the SHR also managed to put out two issues of a newsletter, *Friendship and Freedom*, which became the first known homophile publication in the U.S.

In 1950, the beginnings of what was to become the Old Town Art Fair helped to entrench and publicize the artistic and bohemian climate of the area. Community historian Shirley Baugher states, "The first Art Fair did not begin as an art fair at all. It started in 1950 as a big neighborhood party, and it was called The Old Town Holiday. The first artists were actually party guests: neighbors, friends, volunteer workers, and a few outsiders. Neighbors served as both hosts and exhibitors. Participants displayed their art on fences and tables on Lincoln Park West and its two adjacent alleys.

"The first fair featured the work of 70 artists, and the term 'art' was loosely applied. Exhibitors showed everything from crocheted potholders to high-quality oils and watercolors. We featured only local artists, and now they come from all over the world. It was held for one day only. Neighbors put up their exhibits the morning of the party and took them down at the end of the day..." (Bross, 'Old Town Art Fair: Treasures, Gardens, and Community Spirit.' *Classic Chicago Magazine.com*, June 4, 2017).

Another frequently cited factor for the flowering of the hippie/counterculture movement in the area was the opening of the Old Town School of Folk Music at 333 North Avenue on December 1, 1957. Early legends appearing at the school included Mahalia Jackson and Pete Seeger. The school featured a multitude of lessons—guitar, harmonica, banjo, folk dancing, and more. As a result, the neighborhood saw a rise in performance venues to accommodate all the budding musicians as well as fans of the folk music revival that was sweeping the nation. Though the Old Town School of Folk Music relocated after five years, its influence on the neighborhood remained.

Populated by an abundance of musicians and artists, Old Town was fertile ground for a different set of standards. The area was a site for free speech and new ideas—alternative lifestyles, left-leaning politics, the mystic sciences, alternative religions, and underground newspapers. There were street-corner poets, performers, and orators. Coffee shops and cafes, bookstores, and record stores opened in the neighborhood, catering to the counterculture demographic as well as the tourists and weekend beatniks frequenting the area.

In 1962, a three-story brick building at 1514 N. Wells Street became the first Crate and Barrel store—a new type of retail experience. As the tale goes, after renting the space and purchasing the merchandise, the owners had no money left for shelving units. In a show of marketing genius, the display "problem" became the store's trademark. Crate and

Barrel displayed its housewares merchandise in crates and barrels, often on a bed of packing material.

In 1963, the first Barbara's Bookstore opened at 1434 N. Wells Street on the first floor of a three-story Victorian building with apartments above. The well-curated bookshop became a popular neighborhood spot. On the Barbara's Bookstore website, the first Wells Street shop is described as "... a large, shambling, literary bookstore with creaky wood floors and dust dating back to the early 1950s. The closest thing we had to a computer was a plug-in cash register, pen and paper, and a staff that knew every book by heart." The store eventually expanded to include the second floor. In the years following, Barbara's Bookstore opened several satellite stores throughout Chicago and the suburbs.

In November 1965, Old Town solidified its status as the apex of hipness with the opening of Piper's Alley—Chicago's answer to London's swinging Carnaby Street. The entrance to Piper's Alley was beneath an enormous Tiffany lampshade at 1608 N. Wells. The open-air "mall of mod" was a U-shaped brick back way lined by buildings that housed businesses catering to the young and hip. Piper's Alley featured a candle shop, a bookstore, a store that carried posters, decals, and body paints. There was a glass and trinket shop, a candy store, Charlie's General Store, a leather shop, Aardvark Cinematique, a performance space, a gallery, and assorted eateries. Piper's Alley flourished for five years. Things ended on March 1, 1971, when a fire swept through the alley, damaging the collection of buildings that comprised the "mall of mod."

Donald Bell recalled the Old Town neighborhood of the 1960s. "My parents and brothers and I would come to Old Town from the South Side for fun. North Wells was a wonderful, family-appropriate carnival of weirdness. Paul Bunyan was a big pancake house that had dollar pancakes. There was the Ripley's Believe It Or Not Museum, the original Crate and Barrel, and the Wax Museum. Old Town was a cultural freak show back then."

The Royal London Wax Museum at 1419 North Wells featured 110 figures by Josephine Tussaud. Many of those commemorated in wax had strong Chicago connections—Ernie Banks, Hugh Hefner, Dillinger, and Capone. Assorted display dioramas featured recreations of the Civil

War, the St. Valentine's Day Massacre, and DaVinci's Last Supper. There were wax figures of presidents, generals, as well as television and film stars. The museum had a Chamber of Horrors and another room devoted to fairytale and storybook characters. The Royal London Wax Museum closed in 1987.

"My parents used to take us to Wells Street in the 1960s," said Richard F. "We came to see the Pop Art and to eat at Chances 'R' (1528 N. Wells), where we could eat peanuts and throw the shells on the floor. Even at that age, I had an affinity for the freedom of hippie culture. I remember Piper's Alley and the Day Glo posters and daisy stickers and all that."

Daniel L recalled when his father took him into town from the suburbs and showed the family different Chicago neighborhoods. "We came to Old Town and went to Pipers Alley. My dad pointed out the neighborhood, saying that these were hippies. 'You know what hippies are, right?' Anyway, I remember thinking it was a cool place, and I wanted to come back someday. I did come back to Old Town. After high school, I came into the city one day to find gay life. I wore a suit and platform shoes to meet other gay people. I didn't know where to go, but I remember my Dad taking us to those neighborhoods. I went to skid row and had no luck finding gay life there, but at a newsstand, I picked up a copy of *Gay Chicago*. In the back were maps of the neighborhoods with the gay bars and businesses marked. One of those maps was of Old Town."

"When I was a kid, my parents took me to Bizarre Bazaar and Piper's Alley and the Pickle Barrel," recalled Jaime Krohn. "There was also a place on Wells with the best chicken soup—you ordered it with a half chicken or a full chicken. Those were the choices—it was chicken soup for a family of four."

In the 1972 *Bob Damron Address Book*, no gay bars were listed on North Wells Street, though later that year, the Glory Hole would open. However, the Damron guide for that year does mention that Old Town is a cruisy area for gay men, "...very 'hip,' especially on Sunday afternoons."

By 1974, North Wells Street in Old Town was a destination spot known for its gay nightlife. The stretch was one of several pockets of gay activity on the North Side. What made the North Wells strip unique was the tight concentration of gay nightlife on the east side of the 1300 block. For years, this stretch was a hub of LGBT activity until the area changed again and the block became something else entirely.

1355 N. Wells

On June 12, 1963, the *Chicago Tribune* announced, "A new showplace in Old Town is the Paul Bunyan Cook Shanty at 1355 Wells St. where the capacity is 350 and some other things, including family dinners, are giant sized in keeping with the legends surrounding the giant logging hero of the north woods." The restaurant's name eventually became Paul Bunyan of Old Town with a motto that read, "We have an oversized desire to serve the best food at the most sensible prices to the greatest number of people." The rustic décor of the Paul Bunyan included barrels, huge two-man crosscut saws, wagon wheels, lanterns, and lots of wood. The overall effect gave the eatery its "logging camp atmosphere."

By the end of the decade, the enormous Paul Bunyan space was being repurposed. In 1970, it also became the Paul Bunyan Theater. Productions there included *The American Dream* by Edward Albee, *Hello from Bertha* by Tennessee Williams, and *The Education of H-Y-M-A-N K-A-P-L-A-N*, a musical adaptation of the Leo Rosten stories.

In March 1971, there was an on-site auction of the "rustic antiques" of the Paul Bunyan—wall décor, a wine press, coffee grinder, wagon wheels, bells, lamps, chairs, etc. (Auction notice, *Chicago Tribune*, March 14, 1971).

In 1972, the space became the Brown Shoe Jazz Club with a big brown boot above the entrance. The opening of the club featured performances by Linda Ronstadt and Jackson Browne. During its brief run on Wells Street, the Brown Shoe showcased such varied talents as John Prine, Anne Murray, Weather Report, Donny Hathaway, Todd Rundgren, Dexter Gordon, Pharoah Sanders, the Buddy Rich Band, Woody Herman, and Chick Correa. According to advertisements at the time, live music at the Brown Shoe was usually three, sometimes five bucks, often with a two-drink minimum.

Following the closure of the Brown Shoe, the 1355 N. Wells building underwent renovations. In the autumn of 1973, the single-story brick building was again listed as available for rent. The space was described as "15,000 sq. ft., fully air-conditioned, new front, zoned commercial, lg. washrooms, sprinkler, and alarm system...now suitable for office space, restaurant, or entertainment." (Rental notice, *Chicago Tribune*, Oct. 21, 1973).

While Wells Street was undergoing change, larger cultural changes were underway in the city as well. In Chicago, the youth-driven gay liberation movement was taking firm hold, led by the Gay Liberation Front. "Following the June 1969 Stonewall riots in New York City, a more militant gay liberation organization formed at the University of Chicago. This group sponsored a citywide dance at the Coliseum Annex in 1970, the first public lesbian and gay dance (aside from the annual Halloween drag balls) held in Chicago." (Chad Heap, 'Gays and Lesbians.' *The Encyclopedia of Chicago*, Newberry Library, 2004.)

Two thousand gay folks attended the dance.

The following weekend, gay activists picketed the Normandy (744 N. Rush Street), drastically cutting into the bar's business. The leaflets from the Chicago Gay Liberation Front handed out to the crowd read, "The oppressive atmosphere of the Normandy must be removed. The right to dance, any tempo, any style, is thus a crucial step towards our personal and collective liberation."

Activism brought results. Same-sex dancing was soon permitted in the Normandy. Gay people had come together, organized, presented a unified front, and won. Two months later, the Gay Liberation Front helped organize Chicago's first Pride March. It was a new age for gay folks.

Decades of repression were over. The previous restraints caused a deeper appreciation of things formerly taboo. Sex had been forbidden. Coming together meant being vulnerable. And same-sex dancing was against the law. In a matter of months, all that changed. Pride was power. Coming together brought strength. A crowd was a party. Decadence was good. Outrageous was in. And the underground was above ground. Many gay people wanted to do more than celebrate those new freedoms—they wanted to revel in them. Fun meant drinking, drugging, and dancing. There were still plenty of gay bars, but now gay clubs began to emerge—places where people could spread out, cut loose, and party. Gay folks were literally claiming their space. Gay clubs and discos required more room. The single-story, 15,000-square-foot space with the vaulted roof at 1355 N. Wells Street was available. The enormous space was well suited for what the owners of Our Den had in mind.

Described in advertisements as "Chicago's Decadent Superdisco" and "the Gay Disco of the Future," Our Den opened in 1974 at 1355 N. Wells amidst a flurry of fanfare.

The weeknight schedule at Our Den tended to be as follows— Tuesday was Disco Bash Night with a $3 door charge and free cocktails. A dance contest with a $50 cash prize was the draw on Wednesday evenings. Dance contests were very popular in gay clubs at the time. At Our Den, Thursdays were the most open day of the week. Designated as Event Night, Thursday was the night for outside entertainment or, more often, Movie Night, with plenty of popcorn on hand. Sometimes, on Thursdays, the bar also had Splash Parties. Unlikely as it sounds, Our Den had a large freestanding swimming pool beyond the dance floor towards the back of the bar. Our Den was closed on Mondays but had a 4 a.m. license, so it was open late Tuesdays through Sundays.

After a year in business, the name of Our Den was changed to Den One. During that first year, Jim worked there as a waiter. "...It was a restaurant and bar before it was a dance bar. ...We sold anything from steak to hamburgers to chicken and salads, but it didn't stay a restaurant too long. The restaurant used to be out on the dance floor before it was a dance floor. There was an octagon bar, then under the DJ booth...there was a coat check, there was a stage, then down a long hallway, past the men's and women's bathrooms to the left, there was a little storeroom, which was like an office, then next to that was the kitchen. Shortly after they started being a dance bar, they closed the restaurant. It went from Our Den to Den One." (St Sukie de la Croix, 'Chicago Whispers #217,' *Windy City Times*).

The name change came with several bar improvements as well, including a new sound and lighting system, a remodeled front lounge area, and a bigger swimming pool. For the second anniversary, Den One proudly showcased the new larger pool with the ad copy, "Bigger Pool. More Fun!"

On the website *Redbullmusicacademy.com*, Jacob Arnold writes, "...The club became hugely popular with many of the Black gay party-goers who went to the Warehouse (206 S. Jefferson St.)...The venues were 'sister clubs,' with the Warehouse acting as the after-hours bar for Den One." (Arnold. 'The Den: Ron Hardy's First Year as a DJ.' *Redbullmusicacademy.com*).

Den One ad from Gay Life, September 1976, featuring a lambda.

For their logo, Den One adopted the Greek letter lambda. Den One lambda T-shirts were available for purchase behind the bar for $2. The lowercase lambda became an early symbol for the gay rights movement after being adopted as a symbol by the Gay Activists Alliance.

Gay Activist Alliance leader Phil Raia was present when the decision was made to adopt the lambda as the symbol for the early gay rights movement. "Lambda is the 11th letter of the Greek alphabet, and it means 'moving forward.' A lot of things were talked about as a symbol. We needed one. All the other organizations at the time had one—the peace movement, the women's movement. The lambda symbol was decided on by the executive board of the GAA and then brought to the next general meeting. Everybody ended up embracing the Lambda."

(Keehnen, 'Gay Roots: Talking with early activist Philip Raia,' *Windy City Times*, Nov. 15, 2016).

In 1975, popular nightlife personalities and party-time gurus Mother Carol (1942-1979) and Eddie Dugan (1944-1987) joined forces to cosponsor a new and instantly popular community event, the Mr. Windy City contest. Each gay bar was eligible to hold an open competition and select a candidate to go on to the citywide contest later in the year. Most gay bars in Chicago and the suburbs participated.

As explained in the Mr. Windy City program, "The aim of the annual Mr. Windy City Contest is to bring together a diverse cross-section of the community, allowing the contestants an opportunity to express themselves as to who and what they are and to say to those around us that we are proud of being gay."

The bar community arrived at the Germania Club (108 W. Germania Pl.) that evening, eager for a lively night with plenty of eye candy. They were not disappointed. In the end, 20-year-old Robert Larson, representing Our Den (prior to the name change), was selected as the first Mr. Windy City. In addition to receiving $500 in cash, Larson's prize package included a weekend for two at the Saugatuck Lodges. Entertainers at the first Mr. Windy City contest included Mother Carol, the Bearded Lady, Ebony, Wanda Lust, and Tillie the Dirty Old Lady. Coming out victorious at the first Mr. Windy City Contest gave Our Den the spotlight and a certain amount of prestige. Following the festivities at the Germania Club, there was a party at Our Den to celebrate Larson's victory.

In the essay, 'The Den: Ron Hardy's First Year as a DJ,' DJ Charles Perkins is quoted as saying, "Our Den was a mixed white and Black gay club, which was unusual for Chicago. After its first year, it was renamed Den One and catered to a mostly Black crowd on the weekends." (Arnold, 'The Den: Ron Hardy's First Year as a DJ.' *Redbullmusicacademy.com*.)

Being a mixed gay bar at the time did not make Den One issue free. In 1975, the bar was picketed. *Gay Life* newspaper covered the protest. "Charges of brutality and discrimination have been leveled against Den One...as a result of an altercation there Friday night.

"Jackie Hamilton, 20, a Black lesbian, stated she was confronted by the white female bartender on duty that evening and made the object of racial slurs. Ms. Hamilton said the bartender made threats to assault her. She further stated she got up to leave the bar at the time rather than have a confrontation.

"According to Ms. Hamilton, upon returning to get her purse, which had been left behind, she was assaulted and bodily removed from the bar by Leo Baker, manager of Den One. After Mr. Baker's alleged assault, the police were called, and Ms. Hamilton was placed under arrest on charges of assault and disorderly conduct. Police officers at the scene and their supervisors refused to allow Ms. Hamilton to sign cross complaints against Mr. Baker and other employees of Den One..."

In the *Gay Life* piece, Den One co-owner David Myers stated, "If we are anti-anything, we are anti-troublemakers." He further pointed out that Den One has always maintained an open policy to any member of the community who displays acceptable social conduct.

"At least four employees testified that they received unprovoked assaults from Ms. Hamilton after her alleged conduct made it necessary to ask her to leave.

"Manager Baker countered Hamilton's charges and added that Hamilton was expelled only after she threw objects at employees and became loud and abusive. As a supposed result of the incident, two employees resigned from their positions, being afraid to return to work due to Ms. Hamilton's threats of 'getting even.'" ('Disco Picketed.' *Gay Life*, August 1, 1975).

A 1976 advertisement in *Gay Life* newspaper read, "We are Den One. Where gay Black Chicago comes to cook...and baby, we cook. Den One is people meeting people. Den One is gay-owned and operated, gay men and women invited, a total gay community, all under one roof, experience the best in blended music and incredible lights under the direction of Carmen Adduci."

The distinction of being gay-owned and operated was an important one to make at the time. In Chicago, many of the gay bars from the 1940s through the 1960s had been mob owned. Gay liberation brought an awareness of patronizing our own, keeping gay dollars "in the family," and supporting bars that gave back to the community.

Den One was a club that supported the community. In 1974, a group of medical students founded Howard Brown Health Center in response to the skyrocketing amount of sexually transmitted diseases among gays. Sex was everywhere for gay men, and so were STDs. The new era of gay sexual freedom required a deeper understanding of the patient. Gay men needed the non-judgmental diagnosis and treatment of STDs (STIs). The original clinic opened above a grocery store near Fullerton and Lincoln Avenue, across the street from the Biograph Theater.

In 1976, Den One hosted a dance marathon, and all proceeds went to the fledgling Howard Brown Clinic. The marathon began at 10 p.m. Friday with "continuous dancing until the last couple stops." The winning couple won $500. Fliers read, "Couples will be entered from participating gay businesses and organizations. All couples must be sponsored!" To foster community spirit, DJs from several area gay discos did sets. Prizes were donated by an array of local gay businesses. The staff at Howard Brown monitored the dancers and the event. The $2 door charge was good for the full 72 hours. Continental breakfast and coffee/juice were served at times when the law prohibited the sale of alcohol.

Den One hosted a solid number of events that brought in crowds. The bar was the place to be for Mardi Gras Week, with food, drink, a masquerade ball, and the selection of the royal court. The city kings and queens were crowned at the Mardi Gras Ball.

Ley-Nite at Den One was a Hawaiian Luau when the bar was given a "total Hawaiian atmosphere." The luau included food and drink. Door prizes were another way to bring in a crowd. On Friday nights, Den One had a door prize raffle, and the winner received a cash prize of $100. Saturday was a $100 door raffle night as well. Bottles of champagne were sometimes given as door prizes on weekends. Ten-speed bicycles were also a big door prize at Den One and several other gay bars in Chicago. In the 1970s, ten-speed bicycles became affordable and widely available. The increase in bike riding reflected several things—the nation's current health craze, concerns about air pollution, and rising gas prices. Bike riding also helped give the rider hot legs and a great butt.

In 1976, rumors circulated about a second Den One location on Broadway, but Den Two never happened.

"Den One was a fun place to dance because many times it wasn't just you, it was everybody," recalled Dan H. "The music was so good. I remember being there and everyone doing the same dance—like the hustle or the slide. It was that sort of place. I don't remember doing much more than dancing there, but that and the music was enough."

"The lights around the dance floor were the skeletons of these big umbrellas that had Christmas lights wrapped around them," added Allen Patrykus.

Den One was Mike F's first gay bar. "Den One was a big room with great sound and a packed dance floor. That was also the first time I ever set foot in a discotheque. 'Who's That Lady' by the Isley Brothers was playing. I sat there by the side of the dance floor and saw that the whole crowd was Black. Then a man came and sat down next to me, someone who eventually became a good friend. Anyway, he asked me what I was doing there. I told him it was my first gay club. He said, 'You should go where the white boys go,' and then he told me about Dugan's Bistro."

An ad for Den One, ca. 1975, shows that the bar welcomed a diverse crowd.

Gay Life newspaper reported that the Chicago-based R&B group the Chi-Lites, whose hits included 'Oh Girl' and 'Have You Seen Her,' made a surprise visit to Our Den one evening and lip-synched to a couple of recent releases.

In 1977, the late Jim 'Dottie' Dohr (1950-2010) quit his hotel job to become the assistant manager at Den One, a move that he called "a disaster." As Dohr explained, "Den One was on Wells Street and later became Carol's Speakeasy. I wanted to get into the bar business. I'd had enough of the hotel business. Stella was going to be the manager, and I decided to work with him. Then he got fired, or he quit, or whatever, and I became the manager. I had no idea what I was doing. They let me go within two weeks." (de la Croix, 'Chicago Whispers # 213,' *Windy City Times*).

"They would have a $6 or a $3 cover," recalled Donna Rose in *Last Call Chicago*, "and they'd have an open bar from 8 'til 10, and honey, the children would be lining up, give me six vodka gimlets."

Sheree Anne Slaughter added, "We partied at Den One. Oh wow! When we were doing the Bus Stop, it was a sight! To see the entire floor doing the Bus Stop. It was predominantly a men's bar, but they were friendly." (Karlin. de la Croix. *Last Call Chicago*. Rattling Good Yarns Press, 2022).

An ad for Den One in the form of a coloring book.

Carol's Speakeasy

In 1978, local gay personality Mother Carol (Richard Farnham Carroll) bought Den One and renamed the club Carol's Speakeasy. Since opening her first bar years earlier, Mother Carol had become synonymous with Chicago gay nightlife in the hard-partying 1970s.

Six years prior to taking over Den One and renaming it Carol's Speakeasy, Mother Carol opened her first bar. In 1972, she was already known in the community for her outrageous personality when she took over a little tavern and "turned it gay." The result was Mother's Coming Out Pub at 2519 N. Halsted.

In October 1979, *Gay Life* reporter George Buse wrote, "It was the Coming Out Pub that wound up as Carol's Pub and was the first to offer drinks for 50 cents."

Carol's Coming Out Pub matchbooks, author's collection.

In the piece, Jim Sykes, a friend and patron of the bar, reminisced about the Coming Out Pub. "It was a noisy, raucous place with no air conditioning and a hell of a fun place to party." While running the bar, Farnham became his Mother Carol party persona more fully. Sykes added, "He used to sit on the back bar, crack jokes, and model crazy hats. He also would lip-synch songs. Carol was the only person I knew who could pantomime a whole musical and never know the lyrics," Sykes laughed. (Buse, 'Chicago says goodbye to Mother Carol.' *Gay Life*, Oct. 5, 1979).

Hats became a Mother Carol signature. When it came to headwear, Carol was fond of pastels with ruffles, flowers, and even fruit. At times, her hats were outrageous, but typically, her chapeau style might best be described as Mother of the Bride. The matchbooks for Carol's Coming Out Pub featured a crude sketch of Mother in a "tutti-frutti" hat. In the artist's rendering, a serpentine tongue extends from her open mouth.

"Mother Carol was a renowned celebrity in our community," recalled Arthur Johnston. "She'd had several bars before she died. Sometimes, Pep and I used to go to her bar on Halsted Street. Carol didn't own the place; she was the front person bringing in people. That was a pretty common practice in those days. Carol's Coming Out Pub was Mother Carol through and through. Going in there, we felt that everything was a little out of control. That was the first place where I saw guys dancing on the bar. Then, one of them grabbed the glass ball of a light fixture, and it crashed to the floor, and there was glass everywhere. You just never knew what the fuck was going to happen there. Pep and I like a more controlled space, so we would go there and stay for about an hour, but even that was a lot."

Mother Carol had a larger-than-life personality. She greeted everyone like an old friend. Charisma, a raunchy streak, and a love of the outrageous were all instrumental in her popularity. Debauchery was free-flowing at Carol's Coming Out Pub. People went there to cut loose, carouse, gossip, and drink—not necessarily in that order. The Carol's crowd tended to drink a lot, but not as much as Mother. Free drinks, free rounds, drink specials—Mother Carol was all for anything that kept the party going.

The Coming Out Pub had a jukebox and a tiny dance floor—no more than six feet by six feet. Periodically, the bar put on drag shows. Mother Carol and her sidekick, Miss Tillie aka Tillie the Dirty Old Lady were the usual headliners.

Mother Carol (left) and Tillie (right), photo courtesy of The Gerber/Hart Library and Archives

At the Coming Out Pub, Mother Carol was eager to promote a sense of belonging. For Carol, that sense of community included food. The complimentary Sunday buffet offerings at the Coming Out Pub were actual meals—lasagna, pork and beans, barbequed ribs, and beef stroganoff. Side dishes were a given. At the Coming Out Pub, patrons were treated like family. That welcoming attitude was especially important at a time when more gay openness also meant increased rejection or estrangement from biological families. As a response, many gay people formed their own "chosen families," social groups rooted in acceptance. Farnham was called Mother for good reason.

The bar shenanigans and after-hours card games at the Coming Out Pub often got out of hand, as did the hijinks on the small patio behind the bar. "Visit our famous (infamous) beer garden," read the advertisements.

According to the *Chicago Reader*, "When neighbors complained about the noise and the open sex that took place in the bar's beer garden—Carol's response would be to bellow into the night, 'Mind your own business and pull down your blinds!" (Pick, 'The Queen is Dead.' *Chicago Reader*, Jan. 11, 1980).

As may be expected, several neighbors and the building owner did not get along with Mother Carol.

During the final stretch of Carol's Coming Out Pub, which was open at 2519 N. Halsted, Mother Carol opened another bar, Mother's Other, across the street and up the block at 2548 N. Halsted. However, ongoing conflict with the landlord and squabbles with neighbors led to Mother Carol either being evicted or not being offered a lease renewal. Just as well, Mother Carol was looking for a place where the party could continue uninterrupted and free from hassle.

In 1976, Mother Carol closed both bars and, in September, opened Carol in Exile at 3510 N. Broadway. The bar moved into the space vacated by Garland's, a short-lived gay bar named after Judy. Garland's advertised that it had "Chicago's largest gay beer garden" where you could "roast your own wiener." Garland's had opened and closed earlier that year.

When Carol In Exile opened, *Gay Life* newspaper proclaimed, "Mother Carol is now the First Lady of Broadway!"

MC recalled Mother Carol greeting patrons at the new place. "Standing at the door with one eyelash hanging halfway off, totally drunk, trying to French kiss everyone that walked in the door." (de la Croix, 'Chicago Whispers, *Windy City Times*).

Carol in Exile was a garden-level bar, but despite a new location, new neighbors, and a new name—the hard-partying antics that both defined and doomed her two previous bars were in full evidence at Carol in Exile. At the new place, Mother Carol continued to hold court beside her often-crotchety sidekick, Tillie, the Dirty Old Lady.

Mother Carol and Tillie continued to perform at Carol in Exile, but the shows became more structured. One big reason was that the new place had a proper platform stage. The performance area was to the right as you entered. The regular show at Carol in Exile was called, the Babes on Broadway Revue. The shows frequently starred Mother Carol, Tillie, Amanda Winters, and Mysterious Marilynn, as well as a roster of guest performers.

Ad for Carol in Exile, ca. 1976.

"The stage was on the right when you walked in," recalled Dan Neniskis, "And the lighting for shows were those green, blue, and yellow outdoor floodlights with the heavy glass. That was some harsh lighting."

In addition to her occasional performances at Carol in Exile, Tillie the Dirty Old Lady (1925-2005) was the coat check girl. "Anything that sparkles is Tillie. I'm original. I'm me," as Tillie was fond of saying. A drag performer and bar personality in Chicago since the early 1960s, Tillie was never known for holding her tongue, especially with a few drinks in her. If people checked their coats, it behooved them to leave Miss Tillie a proper tip.

Seven months after the opening of Carol in Exile, on April 2, 1977, a 29-year-old bartender at the place, Frank Rodde, was murdered in his apartment at 3710 N. Pine Grove. Rodde had been stabbed multiple times and left to bleed to death in his bathtub.

Rodde had worked for Carol as a bartender since the Coming Out Pub.

"He was supposed to come to work that night and didn't show up," said Roger Hickey in a 1995 interview with Jack Rinella. "And that was not like Frank. And then they went up to his apartment to check up on him and they found him wrapped in a floor mat in his tub."

Following Rodde's murder, the recently formed Tavern Guild, a collective of local gay bars, began the Frank M. Rodde III Memorial Building Fund. The goal was to raise money for a gay community center in Rodde's name. After two years and countless fundraisers, the Tavern Guild of Chicago turned over operations of the fund, over $80,000 at the time, to Gay Horizons. That meant future donations would be tax-deductible, thereby broadening the donor base. In 1985, the Rodde Center opened at 3223-29 N. Sheffield. In 2007, the community center became the Center on Halsted (3656 N. Halsted St).

Allen Patrykus had a side gig cleaning Carol in Exile in addition to working as a waiter at the popular gay bar Cheeks (2730 N. Clark St.). "One night, while cleaning Carol's bar, I found something," said Patrykus. "In the back of the bar, there was a doorway, and then there was the outside area. I was there sweeping up and taking out the trash and saw the door was slightly open. I looked and behind that door was a bomb. I called 911 and the police came and emptied the building, including the apartments above. Ida Guevarra, who kept Carol's books, lived upstairs, so she was evacuated. Since it was so cold, they let us sit in the back of a police car to keep warm.

"When Mother Carol and her entourage arrived on the scene, she was so concerned about me. She kept saying how sorry she was that I found the bomb. Turns out, the bomb was a scare tactic. It did not have a detonator. Mother Carol was very motherly to me after that. She took me under her wing, and when Mother Carol took you under her wing, she really protected you."

In February 1978, less than a year and a half after opening the doors, Mother Carol closed Carol in Exile. The 3510 N. Broadway space was promptly taken over by Michael "K" (Kucharski) and became the gay bar Broadway Kunfusion for a couple of years. Like Mother Carol, the gravel-voiced Michael K was a popular Chicago gay nightlife personality—a fun host and emcee of the era.

After closing Carol in Exile, Mother Carol worked for several months as a bartender at Cheeks. "When Mother Carol bartended there, she brought a big clientele with her," said Patrykus. In the time that Mother Carol was behind the bar at Cheeks she hosted several popular events, like a sensual banana-eating contest. The winners received a cash prize, free drinks, and a few phone numbers from fans of their technique.

Patrykus recalled one particularly memorable night at Cheeks. "Richard Bubel had worked for Carol for years. He was a spotter. He would come into the bar and order drinks and let her know what bartenders were ripping her off. One night, Richard came into Cheeks to visit Mother Carol. It was raining, and he rode his motorcycle—so he came inside in full leather with a helmet, like my knight in shining armor. I was watching him. He got a beer, came up behind me, and said, 'Mother Carol tells me you have the night off. How about getting out of here with me?' So, I did. Richard and I were together for 41 years until he died in 2019. Later, Richard said that when he asked Mother Carol about me that night, she said, 'Allen will be good for you if you can get him away from running with that young drug crowd.'"

Three months after Mother Carol began working at Cheeks, Ira Jones speculated in his 'Tidbits' column in *Gay Life* that Mother Carol might be buying into the now-shuttered Den One. Speculation was confirmed shortly after with the news item, "Mother Carol is promising a party every night at his private member bar and disco."

"He (Mother Carol) had an opportunity to gain an equity interest in what was then Den One, down on Wells Street, and he went in there as a manager with an equity interest in the place and reopened it as Carol's Speakeasy," said Roger Hickey in a 1995 interview with Jack Rinella.

"Mother Carol took both of us with her when she opened her new place," said Patrykus. "At Carol's Speakeasy, Richard became the head of security, in charge of the 13 doormen stationed in different parts of the bar. And I bartended at Carol's from the day they opened until the day they closed. Mother Carol probably took half the staff of Cheeks with her when she left, or at least a good part of it."

The Carol's Speakeasy facade at 1355 N. Wells St, photo courtesy of Lee Newell.

DJ Greg Collier was another Cheeks employee who came with Mother Carol to the new place. According to Patrykus, "Greg was one of the great DJs. I first met Frankie Knuckles when he would come into Cheeks and talk to Greg about music. They were both so good. If a record wasn't working, they were not afraid to pull it and put something on to get people on the dance floor. Both Greg and Frankie became DJs at Carol's.

"When Mother Carol took over the building, everything was redone. We painted everything brown, and we painted those huge roof trusses black. The ceiling there was very high and bowed. Even those trusses were way up there. It took three or four people just to get the big ladder up. When Carol took over, we redid the placement of the stage as well."

The logo for Carol's Speakeasy became Mother Carol's open mouth with her tongue fully extended. The image was recreated on T-shirts, matchbooks, and assorted club merchandise. Behind the front bar, an enormous 3-D rendering of Mother Carol's mouth with an extended rubber tongue was on display. Three additional oversized murals of the Speakeasy logo were painted on the back wall.

"Mother Carol would lip-synch and dance and vamp it up. His eyes would roll back in his head, and his tongue would lunge out toward the audience. The gigantic tongue became Ma Carol's symbol." (Pick, 'The Queen is Dead.' *Chicago Reader*, Jan. 11, 1980).

Carol's Speakeasy T-shirt with the Ma Carol mouth logo, author's collection.

Gay Chicago described Carol's classic pose as, "...mouth open and flapping tongue extended. We can almost hear her famous phrase, 'Up Your Ass!'"

The logo continued the "tongue-extended" motif that began with the matchbooks from Carol's Coming Out Pub. The Carol's Speakeasy logo was not only slicker, it also reflected mid-1970s queer popular culture. "The Mother's mouth image was influenced by the mouth in *The Rocky Horror Picture Show* (1975) ads," explained Allen Patrykus. "Mother Carol's version was the face she made when she was on stage already blasted, and someone would give her a whiff of poppers. When that happened, she would shriek and sometimes even yell at the top of her lungs, 'Buy all these motherfuckers a drink.' Sometimes, when she said that the place would be packed."

The wooden interior of Carol's Speakeasy was cavernous, with a posted capacity of 1300. Except for the back bar, Carol's was primarily one enormous space. Working with a single room of that size was a challenge. Center Stage (3730 N. Clark St.), the gigantic gay disco in what is now the Metro, had a similar issue. Center Stage devised a tent that was down when there were fewer people and then ascended when the crowd arrived. Carol's Speakeasy didn't have a parachute tent, but the management devised another way to keep the space intimate at slower times.

Lee Newell recalled, "Carol's was one big room, which got bigger as the place got more crowded. There were sliding walls for each bar. There was a sliding wall by the front bar that went away when the dance floor opened. Then, another sliding wall moved away, and the middle area opened. Another wall opened up a bar in the rear part of the bar and then a fourth for that very back bar..."

"We devised these enormous insulated 18' walls on wheels," said Allen Patrykus. "There were six of them, and each was about five feet long and very tall. We used those to close off the back part of the bar early in the evening, and then we would wheel a wall away and the bar could get larger to accommodate the growing crowd until eventually the whole place was open and packed."

Carol's Speakeasy was a membership club. Memberships at the disco and club were usually $5, but the fee was waived on opening night, October 13, 1978.

"I had just come out the year before," offered Rick Karlin. "The Carol's opening was all very exciting and glamorous. Everyone I had ever seen in the pages of *Gay Life* newspaper was there. I came into town for the opening with a few people. We rode in a limo with a bartender at Nutbush City Limits (41 S. Harlem Ave., Forest Park). He was a flamboyant queen who sold furs and could be a nasty drinker. The night of Carol's opening, he was so bad that all of us who rode there with him in the limo took cabs to our cars in Forest Park rather than be in the limo with him for the ride back."

Allen Patrykus and partner, Richard Bubel. The couple helped to open Carol's Speakeasy in 1978 and remained on staff until the bar closed in 1991, photo courtesy of Allen Patrykus.

The wooden exterior of Carol's Speakeasy was painted brown and beige. Above the door line were bricks of a similar shade. There was a slender vertical window on the door. Unadorned block letters spelled out 'Carol's' beside the double doors. The street number, 1355, was above the entrance. Eventually, the Carol's name moved above the doors, and the street number was vertical aside the entrance.

The party could be heard from a block away. Sometimes further. Many nights, there was a line to get inside, but even the line to get inside Carol's Speakeasy was often a party. Inside, the doorman checked IDs. Someone took photos for membership cards. Another person was busy laminating them.

Carol's Speakeasy membership card, courtesy of Lee Newell.

Speakeasy Rules

This card is the property of the issuer and returnable on request. After signing, use of card establishes obligation on the part of the holder to be bound by the rules and regulations of Carol's Speakeasy. Right of entry may be refused due to capacity limitations. Legal ID's must accompany membership card. This card is not transferable and additional ID may be required. If lost or stolen notify Carol's Speakeasy, 944-4226. 1355 North Wells, Chicago.

David Plomin recalled getting his Carol's ID. "I had my perfectly bleached and feathered big hair, but it was so humid outside that after walking from the car and then waiting in line, my hair wilted. So, my ID is of me with wilted hair with the red wall by the coat check as the background."

Entering the bar brought a rush of sensations and smells—heat, sweat, poppers, and stale beer. The advertisements read, "Carol's Speakeasy, Where Chicago Parties," and Carol's lived up to that title for 13 years.

"Carol's was a late-night bar in the days of sex, drugs, and rock and roll," recalled Lee Newell. "Carol's was a lot of everything—a party with a wide variety of men, amazing music, and a great place to pick up guys. Carol's, with the people, environment, and music, kind of reminded me of the raves that came later—just an enormous number of people partying and having fun."

"My boyfriend and I liked to go there to party, do poppers, and dance our asses off," said Del B. "We would dance in jeans and T-shirts, and we usually lost our shirts pretty quickly. Sometimes, I wore a hard hat."

"That was fun, crazy, and wild," recalled Allen, "at the height of gay decadence, gay sexuality, gay freedom, it was fun. She was doing the kind of things that you would think were only being done in New York. Fabulous, exotic stage shows that were very sensual and sexy and trippy and wonderful." (de la Croix, 'Chicago Whispers #81,' *Chicago Outlines*).

The bar made its presence known at the annual Pride Parade. For the club's first float, the staff built different levels onto the back of a flatbed truck. Once the shape was complete, the truck was decorated. A metal arch was added. "There was a swing that hung on the arch," said Allen Patrykus. "That was where Mother Carol sat waving to the crowd in her big floppy hat. There was a cooler of booze on the float that was mostly beer and schnapps, so people got very wasted. I was going around the float on roller skates, handing out helium balloons to people in the crowd. The thing I remember most was how crazy the crowd went when they saw Carol."

When Allen Patrykus was roller-skating around the flatbed, he was also promoting the latest Carol's Speakeasy experience. Two months earlier, in April 1979, Carol's began having Roller Sundays—afternoon roller-skating at the bar. Sunday skating was open to all members, but the afternoons were strictly BYOS—Bring Your Own Skates. Skating was free to members, and those present had free skating access to the flat wooden floor of the cavernous bar. The cocktails flowed on Roller Sundays. Drinking on wheels may not sound like a prudent idea—because it isn't. However, Roller Sunday was the sort of thing that defined Carol's Speakeasy, especially in the early years.

The Carol's Speakeasy float in the Chicago Pride Parade. Photo from the Miss Tillie Papers, courtesy of the Gerber/Hart Library and Archives.

Johno referred to Carol's roller-skating parties as, "drunkenness on wheels."

To prepare for Roller Sundays, the late Richard Cooke (1948-2020) took Mother Carol to a rink on Milwaukee Avenue in Niles. "Skating with Carol was a trip because she couldn't roller skate. I was supposed to teach her. It was my task to keep her falling on me, to make sure she didn't get hurt!"

Greg McFall saw Mother Carol skating. "I was amazed she managed to stay upright."

"She did poppers too," said Joey McDonald, remembering Mother Carol doing poppers while roller-skating. "Mother Carol was there every Sunday with her skates on."

Chicago drag artist Lisa Eaton broke her leg roller-skating at Carol's Speakeasy. At the peak of her career, Eaton was billed as, "more Judy than Judy." Sometimes, instead of Judy, Lisa became Liza. Eaton also did scenes. She was fond of impersonating Tippi Hedren, as well as the attacking seagulls from Alfred Hitchcock's *The Birds*. To achieve this, Eaton screamed, guarding herself against the onslaught of birds with her right arm while self-flagellating with the dishtowel held in her left hand. Eaton performed around Chicago for decades, remaining a fixture on the bar scene until her death in 2002 at age 49.

"At some point, my friends and I stopped going to the Broadway Limited and Carol's became our bar," recalled Frank Nichter.

David Plomin stopped going to Broadway Limited because it was such a firetrap. He was not alone in his assessment. "When I went there, I stood by the stairs. The staircase was wide, but that was the one way up and the one way down from there. And once down the stairs you still had to walk through a room long enough to have two train cars in it before you reached the street. That made me very nervous."

The Broadway Limited (3132 N. Broadway) got its name from a train. When the dance bar opened, the advertisement in *Gay Life* read, "All aboard Chicago's new crack disco! Three levels of dancing, drinking, and lounging! Dine in 1898 railroad cars." At the Broadway Limited, patrons walked through two full-length train cars and up a flight of stairs to get to the stainless-steel dance floor.

Frank Nichter and his friends made their entrance at Carol's at about 11:00. "That was the ultimate time to arrive. I loved it there. Carol's was a good time—a friendly place with everybody just dancing and doing their drugs."

"On Friday and Saturday night, we would always stay 'til closing," recalled Anthony. "Carol would sit and chat with us. One night, she said, 'My cleanup crew can't make it. Would you guys mind staying and cleaning the bar after it closes?' We said, 'Sure,' but once the lights went up, you wouldn't believe what we found on the floor: popper bottles, roach clips, drug paraphernalia, earrings, trick numbers, IDs, credit cards..." (de la Croix, 'Chicago Whispers #187,' *Windy City Times*).

Allen Patrykus recalled the heat generated by the crowd. "At one end of the dance floor were three squared pillars with drink rails. Above the rails, the pillars were mirrored. When the place was hopping, the mirrors would fog, and people would write messages. That was how hot and sticky it was on Carol's dance floor. Those mirrors always went foggy. There was no way the air conditioner could keep up with the heat the crowd was generating. It would be so hot and humid in there that I would be completely soaked with sweat almost every night, my underwear would be too.

"Some nights, David Boyer would come out of the back with a big crate of popsicles on his shoulder and just start tossing them to the crowd, and people would grab them. Or it would be so hot in there that people would run off the dance floor and up to the bar and say, 'Can I just get a glass of water?' Sometimes I'd just say, 'Here girl,' and spray them with water from the spray gun.

"The bar was always busy. I was making drinks from the moment I came on duty until the moment I was off work. The capacity at Carol's was 1300—at least that was what the sign said on the wall, but despite the size of the place, there were nights when you could not move. Sometimes people asked to come behind the bar for a second to have a moment not being surrounded by people."

"As big as Carol's was," offered Dean Ogren, "There were nights there where you could barely move. That place was always the most fun when it was packed to the rafters."

"I liked it crowded, especially the dance floor. When I am dancing, I don't want to be on the stage or on a speaker," said Brian D Smith, "I don't want to be apart from anything. I want to be right in the middle of it all."

Michael Harrington called Carol's a destination spot that was worth the effort. "Parking around there was not easy, but I went because of the dancing, the party, and the atmosphere. My main bar was the Broadway Limited, but I heard about Carol's and went to check it out. I walked in and there was a very large and crowded dance floor. The thing that was apparent to me right away, and something unique for many Chicago bars, was that it was wonderfully integrated—Black, Latino, and Women. The spirit of the place, the staff, and the crowd were all very welcoming. The crowd reflected the ownership and management of the place. There weren't a lot of bars on the North Side that were that way."

"Carol's had a wonderful vibe of people being out and just having fun," said Arthur Johnston. "Some found the Bistro (420 N. Dearborn) a little too fancy. Carol's was more relaxed."

"I liked that Carol's was more of a mixed crowd," said Race Bannon, "Much more mixed than at the Bistro. As a result, the music played at Carol's wasn't all traditional disco. They played different things."

At *redbullmusicacademy.com*, Chicago DJ Danny Goss (1959-2022) recalled. "It was quite a fun club. It was the only thing...as far as gay bars went, that even came close to giving the Bistro a run for its money. It was nothing like the Bistro...if you didn't like the snobbishness or the ultra-chichi attitude of the Bistro, the only other place you could go was Carol's Speakeasy."

Comparisons between the two popular gay clubs were common. David Plomin called the Carol's crowd "more jeans and flannel shirts and T-shirts," and the Bistro bunnies "a little more Lacoste."

Danny K elaborated, "Carol's was playing a lot of the same music as the Bistro, but the clientele was different. Carol's had a more masculine brand than the Bistro."

"The music at Carol's was for people who really wanted to dance," added Daniel L, "Not music to do pretty dances to. That was the Bistro."

Carol's Speakeasy was Norm Cratty's first gay bar. "I was 24. The crowd, the men, the music, the dancing, the sweating...it was a good time as well as a good workout on the dance floor. I was living at Fullerton and Clark back then and ended up as a dancer at Carol's. I remember leaving there at 4 a.m. in my platform shoes and walking home to my place at Fullerton and Clark. Sometimes, friends and I went for breakfast at the Medinah Restaurant (2401 N. Clark). What a blast those days were."

"In those days on the dance floor everyone was shirtless—smoking and drinking and doing poppers," shared Ed Z. "Some were even doing more than that."

Frank Nichter loved Carol's. "I went there for fun. I got my MDA and started dancing. Then I would take my shirt off like half the guys dancing in the place. When I took mine off, I would swing it around my head and let it fly. I left Carol's shirtless plenty of times. The whole place was like this wild circus, especially because I was drinking and doing drugs at the time."

For a while, it seemed that Mother Carol had found the ideal place.

Mother Carol was born Richard Carroll Farnham on August 13, 1942, in Aurora, IL. Richard Cooke described Mother Carol as, "having a voice that was a cross between Fred Flintstone and Ralph Kramden."

Charismatic, chaotic, larger than life, and very messy—Mother Carol knew how to get a party started, make it the place to be, and keep the party going longer than anyone. Those skills, combined with a flair for the outrageous, helped to make Mother Carol the queen bee of Chicago's gay nightlife scene in the hard-partying 1970s.

In 1980, the *Chicago Reader* wrote of Mother Carol, "His signatures were free-flowing booze, lavish buffets, outlandish drag turns and an unremitting need to 'party-party' to use a popular gay phrase.

"...By several accounts, Carol broke open poppers while performing, flaring his nostrils to sniff in the open vials of chemical and letting the drug do its stuff on his dancing feet and flapping tongue." (Pick, 'The Queen is Dead.' *Chicago Reader*, Jan. 11, 1980).

A *Gay Life* ad for Easter read, "Come watch Mother Carol on her Surrey down Broadway to Fullerton, through the park to North Avenue, and then to Wells Street and back to the Speakeasy." This surrey ride was hardly a quiet Easter morning jaunt around the neighborhood. People came out and followed the carriage through Lakeview (Newtown) and Lincoln Park. Mother Carol was feeling no pain whooping it up that morning with a shirtless hunk at her side. Mother was serving her traditional Easter brunch at the bar at 10 a.m. While showing off her Easter bonnet, Mother Carol promised to bring out her "tutti-fruity" hat that coming Tuesday when the scheduled movie at the bar was *Weekend in Havana* with Carmen Miranda.

"The bar community was more unified at the time," said Allen Patrykus. "Everybody was out having fun. Bars were places of refuge and community in a brutal world. Bars meant more to people back then. A gay bar was someplace special because most people could only be themselves when they were there. People often had to hide who they were in the other parts of their lives. The bar was a place of relief, a place to be free from hiding. Working there, I got to know people and I got to know their lives. I got to know what was going on when they would come in and say, 'Girl, I need a cocktail.'"

One evening, David Plomin and a friend were heading to Carol's. "We parked on a side street off LaSalle, and as we were walking to the bar, bunches of people started walking towards us. They were all leaving Carol's. They said there had just been a raid."

On May 12, 1979, undercover police entered Carol's Speakeasy and found open masturbation in a darkened room in the back. One officer reported he'd had his genitals fondled. A 53-year-old maître d' was charged with public indecency, Mother Carol was arrested for keeping a disorderly house, and three other men with disorderly conduct and failing to leave the bar when told to do so. The cops returned the following week to see if the back room was open. The room had been closed for the time being. Seeing that was okay, the police then locked the doors and turned on the lights. Officers told patrons to remain still, they were going to do a head count to check for fire code violations. Tensions came to a head outside of Carol's when patrons were asked to vacate the premises. Staff reported that the cops were abusive verbally and even physically. (Pick, 'The Queen is Dead.' *Chicago Reader*, Jan. 11, 1980).

At the time, gay caucus spokesman Tom Denney was quoted in the *Chicago Tribune* as saying, "[The raids] had dropped off since 1974...But since the beginning of the year, there have been at least 12 to 15 raids on gay bars in the Chicago Avenue and Town Hall police districts.'

"'This activity started when gay people began heavily supporting the Jane Byrne for Mayor campaign,' Denney added, '...The raids have involved entrapment of patrons by undercover police offering money for sex; mass arrests of customers who are not informed of their rights nor told the charges against them; and at times, physical abuse.

"The three most recent raids came in one week. Two of them, one on May 12 and one on May 19, were at Carol's Speakeasy, 1355 N. Wells

St.; the third raid, on May 20, was at the New Flight on Clark Street (420 N. Clark).

"Denney's group claims that several people were beaten by police in the May 19 raid on Carol's Speakeasy. 'One man suffered a concussion, another had his arm ligaments torn,' he said." (Close-up with Jeff Lyon, 'City gays and cops talk over their problems.' *Chicago Tribune*, May 23, 1979).

In a *Chicago Tribune* follow-up piece, Joseph McCarthy, Captain of Chicago Avenue District, asserted, "...One of the alleged victims of police brutality ran head-on into a light pole while trying to run away from police. And the other alleged victim suffered renewed injuries to an arm that had previously been injured."

McCarthy continued, "We acted on complaints from the public and the alderman's office...That's why we investigated. Was I supposed to ignore the complaints? Was I supposed to let somebody burn to death?"

"The back door of the place couldn't be opened. The sprinklers didn't function. There was exposed electrical wiring hanging down. It was dangerously overcrowded. And my men did witness lewd sex acts in the place when they investigated the complaints." (Weirdrich, 'Gays turn heat back on police.' *Chicago Tribune*, June 19, 1979).

According to the *Chicago Reader*, "...When [Tom] Denney and other members of the caucus met with Commander Joseph McCarthy of Chicago Avenue Police District, the commander got mad when asked specific questions about police records of the raids.

"And then he threw us out," Denney added.

"As a result, members of the gay community met at Second Unitarian Church to form an ad hoc committee to address the raid as well as complaints about the police. The result was Gays and Lesbians for Action. To turn up the heat, the committee planned a march to Daley Plaza for June 5, 1979. An estimated 1,500 people came together that day to hear speeches calling for the passage of a gay rights ordinance." (Pick, 'The Queen is Dead.' *Chicago Reader*, Jan. 11, 1980).

Ray Thomas volunteered to help with that 1979 march. "I was at Carol's both nights that they raided it. It was a little confusing because we had just got there, and we were in our corner dancing, and suddenly, the lights...I think it was 11:00-11:30, the lights came up, and the police came in and said, 'We're closing you down, everybody get out.' So everyone started filing out, and a couple of people got into arguments with the police, and they were very brutal...abusive, physically hitting people, and all of a sudden more cops showed up, and people were looking at each other like, 'Let's get out of here,' so we left. [We] tried to get away from the area as soon as possible." Thomas added, "We were going to have a march...and I was one of the volunteers from Carol's because I was one of their regulars. I helped organize, like keeping people in line and walking along the side, and we marched down Clark Street all the way to Daley Center to stop the raids on the gay bars. It was really a growing experience." (de la Croix, 'Chicago Whispers #68,' *Chicago Outlines*).

According to the *Chicago Tribune*, "Mayor Byrne warned police command, '...to root out any unfair police activities in areas popular among gays.

"'...There certainly, in my view, has been harassment in the gay community,' Mrs. [Mayor] Byrne said. 'I think they have rights just as straight people, as they call them, have rights.' (Axelrod, Kozol, 'Byrne, top police call war on drugs.' *Chicago Tribune*, June 2, 1979).

Many felt the psychological toll of the raids and the police harassment. Bonita Brodt did follow up on *Chicago Tribune* reportage, interviewing Ray Hammerberg, one of the Carol's patrons injured in the raid. "'...I get a little nervous, I have to admit, looking over my shoulder and wondering if there's going to be trouble again,' he said, 'I try to stay up near the front, by the exit, so I can leave real quick if I have to.'"

Hammerberg gave Brodt his version of events. "I was dancing that night when all these cops came in through the door...I didn't know what was going on.

"'There was never any announcement or anything that we were being arrested; we were just moved out to the street...I was there with a friend of mine, a freelance photographer for *Gay Life*, and he started to take some pictures." Hammerberg said that police then grabbed his camera, removed the film, and exposed it. "He wasn't giving them any trouble, but they grabbed him and started taking him away.'

Hammerberg wanted to know what was happening. "I followed the officer and asked him where he was going. I said, 'Sir, May I ask what you are taking him away for?'

"'The officer said it was none of my business. Then I said my friend was a photographer and a member of the press and he should be treated as such, and that's when they grabbed me.'

"Ray said one officer grabbed his wrist, jerked his arm behind his back, and pushed it up very hard, so it hurt.

"'He looked at the other officer and said, 'Oh, we've got a little fruit to play with,' and they took turns passing my arm back and forth between them and twisting it...

"Ray was charged with disorderly conduct (the charge was eventually dropped) and was transported to Henrotin Hospital from the police station after he complained of pain in his arm.

"The hospital X-rayed his upper arm and found torn ligaments. He wore his arm in a cast for five weeks." (Brodt, 'Gays fear resumption of the raiding game, the injured party.' *Chicago Tribune*. Feb. 28. 1980).

Though Carol's owner, Frank Kramer, admitted there were some violations (the sprinkler system didn't work, and there were as well some holes in the wall), he considered the raid harassment. "...If it was the code violation that bothered them, they would have come during the day and told us to fix something. There were violations, but that's no reason to stage an all-out raid on the place..."

Mayor Byrne reiterated her stance regarding the raids and harassment of the gay community. "The city will act if there's a violation in a tavern, and that goes for violations of the building and electrical codes, but the city must treat everybody the same." Byrne said, "I told them [the police], 'Don't go find them in one place and let the place across the street go free because it's not gay.'"

Activist and publisher of *Gay Life*, Grant Ford (1939-2019) was quoted as saying, "Relations with the police have improved. ...The harassment is much more sporadic now, and since Byrne issued her order to the police, and some of the police commands have changed, we have developed better working relations."

Ford continued, "...I think police officials now know that we won't tolerate this, that we will rise up in anger if one of the well-known gay bars is harassed. ...We're trying to tell them that we're not going to be second-class citizens anymore and that we expect to be served and protected just like anyone else..." (Brodt, 'Gays fear resumption of the raiding game.' *Chicago Tribune.* Feb. 28. 1980).

A few days after the protest march downtown, Mother Carol took the stage at the Speakeasy. "Carol thanked his customers for supporting the march, promised his bar would stay open, and pledged that the tavern would stand behind its patrons in the event of another raid. 'And now,' he said, signaling for the music, 'it's time to have a great party.'" (Pick, 'The Queen is Dead.' *Chicago Reader*, Jan. 11, 1980).

Though only in his thirties, years of unbridled partying had taken a toll on the health of Mother Carol. The late Richard Cooke recalled visiting Mother Carol at Edgewater Hospital. "Carol had a health scare, a heart incident. Every night, Mother Carol would put away a whole bottle of vodka. She couldn't stop herself. That time, the examining physician told Carol that although she was in her mid-30s, she had the internal organs of a 93-year-old. Carol said, 'Richard, I don't want to die.' And I said, 'Girl, you won't die if you just straighten up. You've just got to straighten up.' Then she said, 'Ok, I'm gonna do better. I'm not gonna drink anymore. I've learned my lesson.' She was going on and on at the time. Of course, none of that was true. As soon as Carol got out of the hospital, she went right to the bar and had a bottle of vodka."

In 1995, Roger Hickey (1935-2012) shared with Jack Rinella, "...Carol had been warned six months earlier that if he didn't take care of himself, he was going to die. He developed jaundice and was really in bad shape. ...He was told that he would have to straighten up, or he was gone. I think Carol made a conscious decision that if he had to alter his lifestyle in any way, give up his partying, it just wasn't fun to him." (Jack Rinella Interview, 1995).

In the 'The Queen is Dead' piece, Michael K explained that although Mother Carol had no liver left, he continued to party. "I'm gay, I'm proud, and I'm going to live life to the fullest—that was his credo."

So, the party continued.

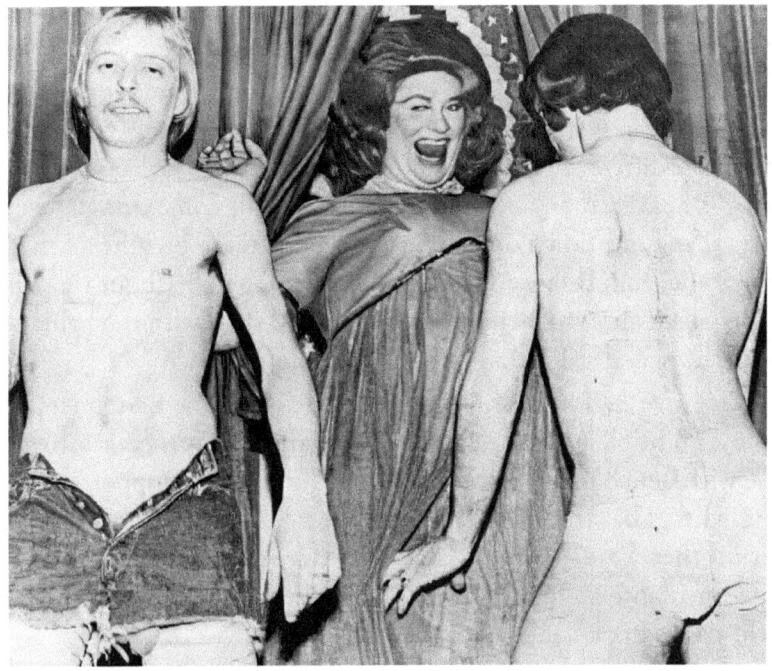

Mother Carol, Queen of Gay Chicago nightlife, photo courtesy of Gay Chicago.

The 1979 Mother's Day Party at Carol's was heavily promoted in *Gay Life*. "Off to grandma's house we go. Ma Carol invites everyone to meet his mother, Lillian, on May 13 from 4 p.m. to 9 p.m. at the Speakeasy. If you come with your mother, she'll get a drink on the house." An accompanying tidbit speculated as to what Mother Carol might serve the ladies for the special buffet. Though hostess of the party for mothers, Mother Carol herself received a good number of floral arrangements on Mother's Day.

Given the meteoric success of the club, Carol's soon had the money and need for renovations that included a new lighting system and a larger dance floor. "The speakers used to be enormous freestanding speakers—huge...five feet high, four feet wide, and four feet thick," said Allen Patrykus. "Those were on wheels. The wheels had locks, but people were always getting on top of those. One security guy was in charge of keeping people off them. We rebuilt the stage. The Speakeasy stage was 25' long, 8' deep, and 4' high. When we redid that, we built the speakers into the frame of the stage." Patrykus added, "It was a high stage and then built into it was a grand piano with a thick plywood cover on top of it, so that part of the stage was a foot higher than the rest of it.

"When we renovated, I also built in a fog machine with dry ice going into a 55-gallon water tank with plywood vents for the steam to come out at three different places around the stage. We did it that way because the fog is heavier than air, so instead of having it come from above and having that come down on people and having them breathe all that, we had it come from below. We tried to get the fog to be about waist-high. All the naked chests dancing with the fog and then with the lights—the crowd, the heat, the music—it was incredible.

"When we redid the stage, the dad of one of the bartenders was a mason, and he changed the elevated front area and turned it into a park scene with benches, a red brick veneer walkway and lampposts with the globe lights. That was when the five globe lights became a bar logo along with Mother Carol's mouth. The pillars around the dance floor were transformed into lampposts as well, with the globes about eight feet or so off the dance floor."

Following the closure for renovations and due to Mother Carol's declining health, another legend in Chicago's gay community, the Bearded Lady (1947-2003), began appearing at Carol's to bring back the crowds. The Bearded Lady, aka BL, was a bear—furry and burly with a full beard and brown hair that reached nearly to his waist. This bear also had a fondness for kimonos and hand fans. Technically, BL was a theatrical dancer, though he really didn't dance. However, he did have a gimmick.

As the music played and BL took the stage, he would shed layers of clothing. He would appear, perhaps in a poncho, his hair festooned with flowers and toys. With a spin and a shriek, BL might remove a poncho to reveal a housedress. As he shed each item of clothing, he would scream with glee, and the audience would scream in response. BL ended his set wedged into a women's one-piece bathing suit. His act was outrageous, but it also resonated with audiences. The joy that came from shedding multiple layers to become your true self was what gay liberation was all about.

At Carol's, BL mud wrestled—but it was really cake mix. An eyewitness account recalls BL licking his opponent into submission. BL also rode with the Carol's Pride Parade float that year, hopping off at several points to walk, kiss, and model his Bride of Stonewall ensemble—a wedding veil, corset, hot pants, heels, and a ruffled parasol. A string of faux pearls danced upon his furry cleavage.

Despite BL's brief time at Carol's, the Bistro was still his home base. And despite her health issues, the Speakeasy was still the domain of Mother Carol.

Mother Carol had been having all-night boat cruises on Lake Michigan since she had Carol's Coming Out Pub on Halsted. Carol often cosponsored the all-night boat parties with Eddie Dugan of the Bistro. On July 13, 1979, Mother Carol hosted an all-night cruise on board the Trinidad that ended at 7 a.m. The cruise was the start of a full weekend of birthday partying—even though Mother Carol's birthday was a full month away. The event was referred to in the press as, "when they floated her out on the lake."

And that was the first night of the party.

Festivities that weekend included a birthday champagne party with free bubbly all night on Saturday, dancing boys, and, naturally, a birthday cake. On Sunday, Mother Carol offered patrons one of her famous buffets, followed by another full-on birthday party starting at 10 p.m. At the party, Tillie the Dirty Old Lady pantomimed 'Hello, Dolly' with Tillie shouting, 'Hello, Carol,' instead.

Norm Crotty relocated to Chicago from Omaha. "The first time I walked into Carol's Speakeasy, I was wearing bib overalls. Mother Carol was at the end of the bar. He gave me a look and handed me poppers and a pair of gold lame shorts. Then he said, 'Put these on and have fun.' So, I did. I took the poppers and the shorts and started dancing.

"After that, whenever my friends visited from Omaha, I always took them to Carol's. They had never had anything like the Carol's experience before—the size of the crowd, the number of hot guys, even the experience of getting groped at the back bar. They had a blast. One of them moved here."

On Valentine's Day 1979, the Speakeasy had a St. Valentine's Day Massacre Party. For the shindig, the bar was transformed into a genuine speakeasy with a 1920s theme. At the entrance, there was a sliding peephole. A password was required for admittance. Inside were flappers and gangsters and the Lady in Red. Fake cops were arresting people and putting them in a "jail." Those arrested didn't have to spend the evening behind bars. They could bribe their way out. Ad copy read, "Ma Capone returns for the 50th anniversary of the heinous deed' as well as 'one free cocktail to all in 1929 period costume." The winner of the best period costume contest received a free dinner for two at a swanky restaurant.

"Mother Carol was Ma Capone and done up in this big blonde wig and a purple dress with a highly dramatic climax involving Ma Capone meeting her hoodlum end on the dance floor—fake blood and all." (Pick, 'The Queen is Dead'. *Chicago Reader*, Jan. 11, 1980).

In April 1979, *Gay Life* ran an ad for a Friday the 13th party at Carol's held in conjunction with the upcoming release of the vampire comedy, *Love at First Bite*. Mother Carol was Mother Dracula for the evening. "The bloodletting begins at midnight, Friday the 13th. Best dressed Dracula receives 'an authentic Dracula cape.'" *The Reader* recounted the evening. "...He was being carted to the stage in a coffin, and when the bottom fell out, the bar went up for grabs."

Carol's Speakeasy became Rydell High for the *Grease* release party with Mother Carol slipping on Eve Arden's old wig, "...decked out as a high school principal in a violet dress, a green scarf, and half glasses draped from his neck." (Pick, 'The Queen is Dead.' *Chicago Reader*, Jan. 11, 1980).

Del B recalls Mother Carol as fun but drunk all the time. "She used to wear muumuus and would dance and lift it over her head. I saw her try to catch hot guys beneath her muumuu a few times."

The late Jerry Pagorek recalled Mother Carol's love of caftans. "She was always running around in a caftan. And if the wig was on, it was crooked."

"On Mother Carol's last birthday, she came out with some go-go boys," said David Plomin. "They had a 12" single of *Happy Birthday*. Mother Carol was holding court at the end of the bar. She was so drunk that night she could barely stand."

"Every time I saw him, he was a drunken mess and fawning over the skinny boys who hung around him," said Rick Karlin. "It was gross."

Mother Carol had tried to stop drinking before. She had attempted to go on the wagon even back when she had Carol in Exile. As Roger

Hickey recalled, "[Mother Carol] had been sober for probably a month, and then when Frank Rodde was found murdered, Carol had another drink." (Jack Rinella Interview, 1995).

Once again, Mother Carol vowed to dry out, but days later, she went on another binge, declaring that it was her 44th birthday. She spent the day "drinking and carousing" at the popular gay Chicago LGBT outdoor gathering area, the Belmont Rocks. Afterward, Carol continued the party at the popular gay bar Crystal Blinkers (3153 N. Broadway), where, "...Someone lined up 44 shots of Southern Comfort, and he downed them in 15 minutes. He was blitzed; he wound up wallowing in a kid's play pool on the disco's second tier, his friends pouring champagne over his head." (Pick, 'The Queen is Dead.' *Chicago Reader*, Jan. 11, 1980).

Frank Nichter remembered another time at Carol's. "They lined up the shots on the dance floor, and she did one after another, all three dozen or whatever, one right after another with the crowd cheering her on. It was insane."

Anthony shared his final memory of Mother Carol. "...She was sitting in the corner of the bar with drink upon drink in front of her. Someone had sent her a camp birthday card, and on the inside, there was a feather. She must have sat there for six hours; every half hour, she would look up at the card and blow the feather, and then she would go back to drinking. Four or five days later, she died. She was a fun, fun person, but it was the booze that killed her." (de la Croix, 'Chicago Whispers #187,' *Windy City Times*).

"She didn't sit at my bar," recalled Allen Patrykus, "but sometimes I would be working, and there would be 20-30 drinks lined up in front of her. Carol tried to take a sip of everyone's to say thank you. Whenever I mentioned concern about her drinking, she would say, 'Don't worry, Honey, I'm fine.' And give me a wink. But she wasn't fine. A few months later, I was going to Edgewater Hospital to see Mother Carol when she was dying. In fact, I saw her right after they delivered the news to her that she was dying and would never get out of the hospital. A few days after that, she was gone."

On Saturday, September 29th, Mother Carol slipped into a coma. She died at 9:30 p.m. on Sunday, September 30, 1979, at Edgewater Hospital. Mother Carol was 37. The official cause of death was pancreatitis.

The publisher of *Gay Chicago*, Ralph Paul Gernhardt (1934-1989), was quoted as saying, "[Mother Carol] was dedicated to making people happy and achieved his goal through warmth, love, and a touch of tacky zaniness." (Pick, 'The Queen is Dead.' *Chicago Reader*, Jan. 11, 1980.)

Longtime friend Ida Guevarra was also quoted in the Pick piece. "Sometimes he'd be drinking, sitting at the bar, and you'd see tears coming out of his eyes. You'd ask him what was wrong, and he'd say, 'Nothing, nothing.'"

In *Gay Life,* Marge Summit (1935-2023), owner of the LGBT bar His N Hers (944 W. Addison), recalled Mother Carol. "I can't think of the right word for him, but it stands for someone who made people laugh and who showed the gay community that you don't have to be young and beautiful and well built, but you have to have a personality. He had a dynamite personality. ...He was a guy who wanted the world to laugh and have fun."

In the same piece, Joe Nicosia shared, "Mother Carol had more employees than anyone. She was always helping somebody down on his luck. If you ever had a problem, she had a shoulder to cry on. That's how she came to be known as Mother Carol. She carried everyone's problems on her shoulders, and they were big shoulders." Nicosia added, "She helped a lot of gays come out of the closet." (Buse, 'Chicago Says Goodbye to Mother Carol.' *Gay Life*, October 5, 1979).

Ron Helizon (1945-2011), also known as the Polish Princess, celebrated Mother Carol in his *Gay Life* column. "Chicago's gay community was saddened Sunday night by the news of the death of one of the city's top showman and personalities—Richard "Mother Carol" Farnham. It was a fitting tribute as gay bars across the city stopped to remember Ma Carol, for it was in the bars that Carol made his name. We all have memories of this burly Irish guy who seemed to celebrate St. Patty's Day every day. Carol did it his way through all his ups and downs, and when things were not going well, he was always able to come up with a bigger and better idea. At a time in my life when all seemed hopeless, I wandered, frightened and lonely, into a bar called the Coming Out Pub. There, I met people who encouraged me and made me believe in myself. I met one of my closest friends there—Frank Rodde. Who'll ever forget Ma Carol in outrageous hats tossing napkins off the bar or the Sunday buffets, Tuesday 50-cent nights, and Polish hops? Chicago's love affair with Mother Carol began there on Halsted Street, and he went on to steal the show wherever he went. By no means was he perfect—none of us are. Carol knew how to take it and how to dish it out. But wherever he appeared, crowds were sure to follow. Mother Carol touched us in ways we won't soon forget. The thought of a Chicago without Richard Carroll Farnham brings tears to my eyes."

Mother Carol was waked at Blake-Lamb Funeral Home, 1035 N. Dearborn, on October 2nd. As a fitting farewell to the gay nightlife maven, the crowd at the funeral home was well over capacity. As Allen Patrykus recalled, "There was a traffic jam all around the funeral home with bartenders and bar owners and wait staff and customers and others there to pay their respects. They spilled out onto the streets and the sidewalk." In lieu of flowers, donations were made to the American Association for the Study of Liver Diseases

Ronald Kennedy lived in Indiana but drove to Chicago to come to Carol's Speakeasy. "I drove in one night and went there, and there was a sign on the door that said Mother Carol had died. It gave the address to his wake. I thought it was a joke, so I went. It was true. He was dead. I went home on the train speechless."

The funeral was two days later in Aurora.

The following week, the Chicago gay papers published a full-page letter. "The family of Richard Farnham, known as Mother Carol to his many friends, wishes to thank you for your great concern and prayers during his illness and death. We feel he loved you all very much and would want you to remember him as he was—a thoughtful and loving person." The letter from the family was signed by his mother, Lillian, and his sister, Pat.

Following his death, it came to light that Mother Carol had recorded a statement to the FBI. On the tape, Mother Carol recounted to agents about being approached with demands for protection payment.

Summarizing Mother Carol's statement to FBI agents. In mid-November 1978, Mother Carol stated he received a phone call from Frank D, aka Babe, who asked Carol to meet him at Carton's Restaurant (21 E. Chestnut). Upon meeting, Babe claimed to be upset with Carol because he did not get approval to operate Carol's Speakeasy. Babe said the bar was in 'Ceasar's' district and that Mother Carol needed to do the right thing. Babe said they wanted $1,000 per month from the Speakeasy. Babe said the protection money included keeping others from extorting from the bar. Babe claimed it was good he interceded since 'they' wanted to take Farnham for a ride. Babe said 'they' could be rough and would have busted up the bar. Babe wanted payment by December 15, 1978. In the statement, Mother Carol also says he was visited by Peter, another man claiming to be a friend of Babe's. Peter asked about the owner of the Glory Hole and the amount of business that was done there. Mother Carol was also asked about the owner of Alfie's, 900 North Rush St. (Baim, Keehnen. *Jim Flint the Boy from Peoria*, Prairie Avenue Productions, 2011).

In 1995, Roger Hickey shared, "...Once Carol and the two other guys went into the office. I guess they were in there for about a half hour. And Carol came out...these were two guys that I recognized immediately as not being your run-of-the-mill beer salesmen or something of that sort. I would guess that they were mob...As I said, when Carol walked out of the office, he was very angry, very hostile, and very loud, which Carol could do. Those guys picked up their stuff and left. And that was that. It was very, very tense in there; Carol was very shaken by the experience and shaking physically..." (Jack Rinella Interview, 1995).

The situation certainly caused additional stress for Mother Carol, who was already facing grave health issues. Soon after speaking with FBI agents, Mother Carol was gone. However, at the Speakeasy, the Chicago gay nightlife pioneer was still present, at least in spirit.

"As you enter Carol's, above the rack of gay newspapers, there hangs a black and white photograph of Richard Farnum in drag. He is carrying on in the picture, taken several years ago at a Mr. Windy City contest. His tongue is pressed onto the roof of his wide-open mouth, and his nostrils are flared." (Pick, 'The Queen is Dead.' *Chicago Reader*, Jan. 11, 1980).

As Mother Carol would have wanted, glasses were raised in his honor, people came together to celebrate his life, and with little interruption, the revelry continued. A mere two weeks after Carol's death, the Speakeasy celebrated its first anniversary—and the blowout was no memorial. The anniversary celebration was a party that made it abundantly clear why Carol's Speakeasy was the place to be.

"A tall man in a wool sweater is necking with a man in a silk shirt slit open to the waist, their tongues embracing across the gap between their open mouths. Now, the man in the sweater slides his hand ever so slowly down his lover's well-muscled and matted chest, kneading the skin en route. When the massage ends, the lover slips from his mate's grasp and marches to another acquaintance. He slides his stiff hand underneath the new man's crotch in a razorlike motion, and the new man arches his back in a shiver of pleasure.

"In the vicinity, a bare-chested man in a top hat fiddles with the ring jutting from his pierced nipple. He's watching the female impersonators who perform on Carol's raised stage. First, there's one wearing a crimson dress and black underwear, and then another riding a hobby horse. The cowgirl, with frizzy hair and a fringed vest, is rewarded with dollar bills from the audience...

"One female impersonator follows another, all working feverishly to the incessant disco music. A mirror ball sprays dots of light over the dance floor; then the chaser lights go on, then the spinners, then the strobes. The dancers—many touching, some shirtless—gyrate with abandon while other intriguing actions transpire quietly in the shadows. Off to one side stands a guy in black satin pants, his pectorals underscored by sequin half-moons. Eyeing him is a man nude but for a black jockstrap and a ring of paint around each nipple..." (Pick, 'The Queen is Dead.' *Chicago Reader*, Jan. 11, 1980).

"The music was decent, but the place was a dump," said Ronald Kennedy, "and people sure loved to party up a storm there. On the one-year anniversary of Carol's Speakeasy, I met a man there and went back and met him there again five days later. We have been together since meeting at Carol's first-anniversary party."

In March of 1980, Joey McDonald was home from the Navy. "I went to Carol's to meet my uncle and his partner. The drinks were very cheap. That night, I met my best friend, Ray Ray Thomas. It was magical. I had found my twin. We even went to the same school. Meeting Ray Ray at Carol's was how I met many friends and entered the community in

Chicago. Ray Ray also knew the Chicago bop. We had so much fun dancing. That night was our first dance together."

Chicago Molly (Larry Berlandi) was a popular bar personality who opened and closed his place, Molly's Follies (2568 N. Clark), in 1980. In the aftermath of Mother Carol's passing, Chicago Molly came in to help run the Speakeasy.

In 1995, Roger Hickey shared, "Molly was originally from Oak Park. A big guy who did a lot of drag, emceeing for shows, and benefits. He was a very likable guy. He had a lot of charm, and he was the one that assumed the mantle, if you will, for Carol's Speakeasy for maybe two years or three years." (Jack Rinella Interview, 1995).

Ron Helizon said of Chicago Molly, "She [Molly] was like Mother Carol, she was heavy, and she did drag. She was in the mold of Michael K. (Karlin, de la Croix, *Last Call Chicago*. Rattling Good Yarns Press, 2022).

DJ/VJ Grant Smith sometimes had a hard time with Chicago Molly when he was at Carol's. "We butted heads. Molly wanted me to play all the old disco stuff, and I felt that was all kind of over and passé. It was time to move on. I was into New Wave. But at the same time, nothing packed the dance floor like 'It's Raining Men' by the Weather Girls."

Molly tended bar at numerous Chicago gay bars and clubs, including Cheeks, the Lucky Horseshoe (3169 N. Halsted), and the down-and-dirty L.A. Connection (3700 N. Halsted). Chicago Molly also performed and emceed events at other gay venues around town. Chicago Molly died of AIDS on May 9, 1993 at age 45.

Eventually, Roger Hickey bought out Chicago Molly as half-partner of Carol's Speakeasy. "When Roger bought into the bar," explained Allen Patrykus, "and brought in David Boyer, they were the best things that ever happened to Carol's. For example, David was nice enough to come around to the different bar stations during our shifts to make sure all the bartenders got pee breaks; otherwise, there would be no time for anything. I quit smoking when I worked there because I never had time to smoke."

Chuck P. Kass remembers Patrykus behind the bar, "And a few times a night or every once in a while, Allen would ring a fireman's bell and yell, "Everybody salsa!"

Patrykus is unsure when or why the fireman's bell thing began. "Mother Carol had that bell with her at all her places. I don't know if she originally rang it when drinks were on the house or what. It was a nice fireman's bell, probably a foot across at the bottom. The clacker was huge, and the thing probably weighed 20 pounds. At Carol's Speakeasy, it hung above the bar on a chain from the high ceiling with a rope attached to the clacker. When the place was hopping and Larry Fox had the crowd jumping, I would grab that rope sometimes when I was at the register. I'd do it in time with the music and yell, 'Everybody salsa!' I rang the bell when I was feeling it in the moment." Patrykus added, "Eventually, the bell developed a crack and started to fall apart. After the bar closed, David Boyer had it in his basement for years. Then he gave it to me, but by then, the cracked piece had fallen away, and the bottom rim was coming apart. I kept it in my basement another 15 years, but the bell eventually got thrown out a few years ago."

One possible explanation for Mother Carol's attachment to the bell may have been Carol's sometime favorite song. Carol loved 'It Shoulda Been Me,' but she was also especially fond of Liza Minnelli's version of the Kanter and Ebbs tune, 'Ring Them Bells,' from the 1972 television special and bestselling album, *Liza with a Z*. Having the bell on the premises may have been a reminder to Mother Carol to live life to its fullest.

The Carol's Speakeasy's DJ roster was exceptional from the start, with one legendary name after another. Each man in the booth was unique, yet each knew how to get the dance floor jumping. The 1979 DJ schedule at Carol's included Peter Lewicki on Thursdays, Frankie Knuckles in the booth on Fridays, Greg Collier spinning on Saturdays, and Mike Graber getting the folks on the floor on Sundays.

The late Larry "The Doctor" Fox was a favorite DJ of Patrykus, "Foxy was very House. He adopted Frankie Knuckles' form of music and went with it and took it in his own direction."

"Larry Fox was a hardcore partier and a terrific DJ," recalled Chuck P Kass. "You could go right up in the booth and make requests. He was a great DJ because he knew how to work the crowd from beginning to end."

"Carol's was where I met Frankie Knuckles and some great DJs," recalled Diana McKay, a popular Diana Ross impersonator of the time. "Sometimes they even gave me Diana Ross music before it was officially released, so when Diana Ross released the song, a couple of people would come up to me and say, 'I heard Diana Ross singing your song.'"

Tom Parks (left) and Frankie Knuckles (right, photo courtesy of Gay Chicago.

Frankie Knuckles (1955-2014) worked as a DJ in New York before relocating to Chicago and became the resident DJ at the Warehouse (206 S. Jefferson). Knuckles also had DJ gigs at several clubs around town, including Cheeks, Annex II (430 N. Clark St.), and Carol's Speakeasy. Knuckles had a profound impact on the music world, primarily through originating and popularizing the genre known as house music. In 2004, the City of Chicago named Jefferson Street between Monroe and Van Buren—Honorary "Godfather of House Music" Frankie Knuckles Way. The West Loop site was chosen for its proximity to the Warehouse. The three-story loft building at 206 S. Jefferson, which housed the Warehouse from 1977-1982, was designated a historic landmark in 2023.

Malone Sizelove went to Carol's Speakeasy for the music. "Carol's had great DJs, Ralphie Rosario, Freddy Dane, Oscar McMillian. We used to hang out in Gramophone Records (2843 N. Clark St.) on Saturdays and watch our DJ friends come in and buy their music. A big reason for going to Carol's was to hear records and mixes that we couldn't afford to buy."

In 1982, Carol's dance floor was augmented with a light and laser show. The 1970s were over, and the 1980s were here to stay. VJ Grant Smith ran the new light and sound systems with DJs Joel Levin and Larry Fox.

"Back in those days, people came to bars to see new lighting or sound effects, and we would advertise them when they happened," shared Allen Patrykus. "And the DJ would coordinate the unveiling of this new lighting effect on Saturday nights and build to it throughout the evening. People would show up to experience that sort of thing."

DJ Mark Hultmark started at Carol's around this time after the closing of the gay leather dance bar Ozone (112 W. Hubbard), where he had been working. Hultmark was a resident DJ at the Speakeasy from 1983 to 1985. "Carol's was a great place to work," he recalled. "The DJ booth was in a great spot. You could see the dance floor and most of the bar. When I came there, Grant Smith was the VJ, so he taught me that side of the business."

"I was brought in 1982 to run the film program on Sundays," said VJ Grant Smith. "I think at the time, I was working at Coconuts (5320 N. Sheridan Rd)."

Movie Night at Carol's had been going on for years. In the pre-VHS world, Movie Nights were a huge draw. Many Chicago gay bars had a designated evening for showings, which at the time meant using 16mm movies in a film can, threading the reel, using a projector, the whole bit. The Gold Coast (501 N. Clark St.), Carol's Speakeasy, Broadway Limited, the Bistro, and the Glory Hole all had movie nights. The bars tried to coordinate the screenings to avoid conflicting schedules.

The feature films shown at Carol's Speakeasy included *The Ritz, Some Like It Hot, Alien, Amarcord, Meet Me in St. Louis, Desperate Living, the Aristocats, The Producers, La Cage aux Folles, La Cage aux Folles II, The Seven Year Itch, Midnight Cowboy, Fame, 9 to 5, American Gigolo, Sunset Boulevard, Time Bandits, Airplane, Towering Inferno, The Women, Harold and Maude, The Howling, Night of the Living Dead, the*

Lion in Winter, Dragonslayer, Boys in the Band, King of Hearts, Up in Smoke, Clash of the Titans, the Graduate, and even *Bugs Bunny Superstar.*

"Early on, the films were shown in the back bar," recalled David Plomin. "There was a serve-yourself popcorn cart back there. There was some messing around during the movie. Off the back bar, where the movie was playing, was an adjoining room that was completely dark. Some guys liked to slink in there during the movie and mess around."

"I remember thinking it would be a good idea to go there to see *2001: A Space Odyssey* on acid with my boyfriend," said Patt Batt. "I remember the film broke, but I can't remember if they fixed it or not."

David Plambeck recalled Sunday Movie Night. "I saw *Stormy Weather* and *Flashdance* there. We would sit in folding chairs and watch the movie with our libations under the chair."

"As I recall," added Grant Smith, "The three most popular films we showed were *Mary Poppins, Pink Flamingos,* and *The Rose*—in that order, but people also showed up in droves for *Whatever Happened to Baby Jane, Auntie Mame,* and *All About Eve.*

"Because we had those membership cards, and Carol's was listed as a private club and not a bar, we could rent Disney movies. The usual place we used was Films Incorporated. They had professional prints, so the image was great. Sometimes, we used other distributors."

Prior to the movie, Smith started running *I Love Lucy* episodes. The crowd loved it. "The movie night was usually over around 9:30, so I just started playing music. Then I started doing specific edits for specific songs—matching clips from movies and things and synching them to the songs.

"They [the management] asked me what I thought the bar needed. I was very clear about how movie night could go further with the booming video craze. They were very receptive. So, I had them install a video projector above the dance floor, and then we painted the opposite wall white. That was where we projected movies and then music videos.

"When all that was getting done and the scaffolding was up, I got up there and cleaned the ceiling. After cleaning the varnished wood, it actually looked great. When I came on, Carol's had strings of colored rope lights hanging around the edge of the dance floor. While the scaffolding was there, I took the dozen or so strings of rope lights and made them into a V-shape on the ceiling. It looked really cool against the varnished wood. Carol's also had all these red lights everywhere. I replaced them with purple ones. No real reason. It just felt it was time for something different."

CAROL'S SPEAKEASY
Video-Disco Playlist

JUNE 15, 1983

VIDEO TOP 20

1. FLASHDANCE - Irene Cara*
2. LET'S DANCE - David Bowie
3. SHY BOY - Bananarama
4. SO WRONG - Patrick Simmons
5. ELECTRIC AVENUE - Eddie Grant
6. ALWAYS SOMETHING THERE-Naked Eyes
7. BLINDED BY SCIENCE-Thomas Dolby
8. SEX - Berlin
9. COOL PLACES - Sparks
10. SWEET DREAMS - Eurythmics
11. DRIVE ME WILD - Vanity 6
12. BLUE HOTEL - Lene Lovich
13. BLIND VISION - Blancmange
14. FASCINATION - Human Leauge
15. DR. DETROIT - Devo
16. IN MY SYSTEM - Robert Palmer
17. TOO SHY - Kajagoogoo
18. NOBODY'S DIARY - Yaz
19. TEMPTATION - Heaven 17
20. HIGH LIFE - Modern Romance

VIDEO ALSO SHOWING

LOVE IS A STRANGER - Eurythmics
BAD BOYS - Wham
ADVENTURES IN SUCCESS - Will Powers
BEAT IT - Michael Jackson
GET THE BALANCE RIGHT-Depeche Mode
SOLITAIRE - Laure Brannigan
TELEPHONE OPERATOR - Pete Shelley
WISHING - A Flock Of Seagulls
KISS ME - Tin Tin
DON'T TALK TO ME - Altered Images
CHINA - Red Rockers
STRANGER IN DISGUISE-New Models
ANIMAL SONG - Europeans
SIGN OF THE TIMES - Belle Stars
OUR HOUSE - Madness
HIP HOP BE BOP - Man Parrish
ALL LINED UP - Shriekback
LOVE ON YOUR SIDE-Thompson Twins
DER KOMMISSAR - Falco
NEW YEARS DAY/TWO HEARTS - U2
JEOPARDY - Greg Kihn Band

DISC TOP 20

1. BLUE MONDAY - New Order
2. SHOT IN THE NIGHT - Paul Parker
3. BURNING UP - Madonna
4. THESE MEMORIES - Oh Romeo
5. PARTY - Julius Brown
6. WANNA BE STARTIN SOMETHIN-M. J.
7. SHE WORKS HARD - Donna Summer
8. ANGEL MAN - Rhetta Hughes
9. EL WATUSI - Rags & Riches
10. AGAIN & AGAIN - Nikki Lauren
11. I'M FREE - Celi Bee
12. YOU CAN HAVE MY LOVE-Paul Parker
13. I'M ALIVE - American Fade
14. SEARCHIN' - Hazell Dean
15. THE NIGHT - Azul Y Negro
16. MEMORY - Menage
17. STAY WITH ME - India
18. SO MANY MEN - Miquel Brown
19. LET NO MAN PUT ASSUNDER-1st Choice
20. SAFETY DANCE - Men Without Hats

DISCS ALSO PLAYING

LOOK AT THAT BOY/GOIN CRUSIN-Malibu
LOW DOWN DIRTY RHYTHM-Sarah Dash
TAKIN IT STRAIGHT - Cori Josias
OVERNIGHT SENSATION - Peter Brown
USE ME LOOSE ME - Paul Simpson
WHEN BOYS TALK - Indeep
BABY DOLL - Girls Can't Halp It
PUTTING ON THE RITZ - Taco
STOP - Vellery Allington
LOVER TO LOVER - Joe Yellow
I LOVE YOU - Yello
SUMMER DREAMS - Queen Samantha
GAME ABOVE MY HEAD - Blancmange
DANCE FOREVER - Gaucho
I LOVE YOU SO - Mannys
NIGHTLIFE - Lisa
ELECTRICITY - Asheye
FACE TO FACE - The Twins
I DON'T WANT TO TALK-Pamela Stanley
I JUST CANT BELIEVE-Boys Town Gang

Carol's Speakeasy · 1355 N. Wells · Chicago
GRANT SMITH, VJ/DJ
(*- The FLASHDANCE video was edited by Mike Graber)

Carol's Video-Disco Playlist for June 15, 1983, courtesy of Grant Smith.

Change was in the air. MTV and the music video craze were sweeping the nation, transforming the club world overnight. By late 1982, Carol's Speakeasy had gone from being a disco to being a video disco. Soon, advertisements for Carol's in the gay press proclaimed, "Music Never Looked So Good. See Your Favorite Artists LARGER THAN LIFE on our movie-size video screen! The Weather Girls, Phil Collins, Sylvester, Culture Club, Devo, Madonna, Diana Ross, Toni Basil, Wham!, Thomas Dolby, Pointer Sisters, Michael Jackson."

At Carol's, Thursdays became New Video Night.

Tim G remembers the video screens. "I went there mostly at the start of videos. By then, I had experienced men and all that, so when I went to Carol's, my focus was on the new thing—music videos. They played 'Take on Me' by A-ha and Madonna, and I remember hearing 'Thriller' by Michael Jackson there a lot."

When Grant Smith came on board in 1982, Movie Night needed a shot in the arm. Previously, Movie Night at Carol's had been hosted by Hedda Lettuce—not *the* Hedda Lettuce, but an early 1980s Chicago bar personality with the same name.

Arthur Johnston recalled, "Hedda worked at Carol's as a bar back, and sometimes I would need beer or whatever, and Hedda would be down there in the basement and come back with a new outfit crafted from garbage bags."

"I worked at a plastic bag factory at Diversey and Ashland, and I had access to all different colors of plastic," said Allen Patrykus. "I started bringing excess plastic to work and Hedda asked for more. Then she began making outfits out of them—but plastic is extremely hot to wear, especially in a sweaty bar."

"Hedda was also on the softball team," recalled Johnston. "I still remember Hedda coming to practice, but Hedda never called it that. Hedda called it rehearsal. When Hedda showed up for the game, she wore dark green opera gloves that went past her elbows. But actually, Hedda was a tremendous ball player."

Paul Mikos played softball for Carol's for a couple of years. "Before he opened Sidetrack, Arthur Johnston was teaching school and bartending at Carol's part-time. He was our softball coach. Arthur was an incredible coach. He gave equal time to everyone, brought out the best in each player, and fostered camaraderie on the team. We were always in the playoffs, but at the same time, it was never too competitive. After Sidetrack opened, I followed Arthur and played for the team there."

Carol's Speakeasy softball coach, Arthur Johnston, on the ball field, photo courtesy of Bill Miller.

"We had a lot of team spirit," explained Johnston. "We didn't always win, but we all got along well, and once we got out there, we had fun. P.E. was always a terrible thing for me growing up—last picked and all that. When I started teaching, I was working at a school that was very exclusive. The classes were about eight students each, but part of the deal was that I had to coach something. So, I started coaching soccer. When I came here and got with Pep, I used to look at the softball standings in the paper. I made a point of going to games. I did not like having that phobia of sports. I wanted to change that.

"After working at Carol's for a while, I noticed they didn't have a ball team. They said, if you want to coach the team, it's yours. That's how I started coaching 16" softball. Sixteen inches was urban ball, made for the city. A 16" softball could not be hit that far. I was determined to learn all about coaching softball. The training was very on-the-job," explained Johnston. "And everything I learned about gay politics in Chicago, I learned coaching gay softball," he added with a laugh.

"Those Sunday games were rough. Many folks on the team worked with me on Saturday nights—we closed at 5 a.m., and in a few hours, we had to be on the field to play ball. On more than one occasion, I had to rustle up our ball players from Man's Country (5015-5017 N. Clark)."

Carol's was Arthur Johnston's first job in a gay bar in Chicago. "Pep has been in the business since I met him. We had been together since 1973. He was still in the bar business, and I was teaching out in Wheeling and waiting tables at night at a place on Armitage. The manager of Carol's came into the restaurant while Pep was there, and Pep asked if he thought I would work out at Carol's. That's how my crazy life in the bar business all began. Carol's was a good place to start. Carol's had a wonderful vibe of people being out and just having fun. I was there until we opened Sidetrack. I left Carol's in January, and we opened Sidetrack in April."

On Sundays after softball, Carol's offered a complimentary buffet. The pool table had a special wooden cover, a tablecloth was added, and meals were served buffet style.

"After the game, we went back to Carol's to cruise and dance and party," said Paul Mikos. "Sundays were also movie night, so that was going on too, and a buffet."

"I remember hot dogs and big tins of baked mostaccioli with potato salad and bread," said David Plomin. "The Sunday buffet was always a solid meal. Lasagna, salad, garlic bread…"

BBQ ribs, "Mexican Feasts," and lasagna were also popular meals. The main requirements for the food at Carol's was that it be easy to serve and hearty enough to feed an enormous crowd.

"There were tacos a lot," recalled Jeffrey Pool. "We used to come there after the softball games, and there was always plenty of food."

Mark Hultmark recalled the buffet. "I remember being in the DJ booth with a plate of pork chops, mashed potatoes, and green beans. Sometimes, they had chicken. The food there was good stuff."

"Cesar was in charge of the buffet," said Rick Karlin. "Ribs and baked beans, sometimes he even had a champagne buffet." Cesar Vera was not only the chef at Carol's, but she also sometimes performed there as well. Cesar was a longtime bartender at the Loading Zone (46 E. Oak) as well.

Lori Cannon shared, "Cesar was a throw caution to the wind kind of gal and a show unto herself, but that era of Carol's was a different time.

Years later, I got to know Cesar again when she ended her career as a social worker for Heartland Alliance."

The Carol's Speakeasy store, photo courtesy of Jimmy D'Ambrosia.

Carol's Kitchen opened in July 1979 and was run by Vera. The kitchen offered menu selections—full entrees, hot and cold sandwiches, and daily specials. The kitchen was open for business four days a week, 7 p.m.-2 a.m.

"The kitchen part of Carol's with hot sandwiches and all didn't really work out," explained Allen Patrykus, "but the free Sunday buffets were extremely popular. For a while, after the menu kitchen closed, there was a juice bar back there that served about 20 different canned juices, but that didn't last very long."

"The walk-in cooler back there was enormous," added Patrykus. "If you put a case of beer in that cooler, it would be ice cold in minutes. Four big ice machines were back there, as were our dressing rooms. The main dressing room was where we all got ready, mostly just changing into our Carol's shirts and making ourselves beautiful. The dressing room had a mirrored wall and a full-length dressing table. Sometimes, when people had breaks, they would go to the bathroom and then the dressing room to do a bump before they went back to their station. We didn't really keep things in the dressing room. Most people had a backpack or something that they kept underneath the bar where they were working.

"The smaller dressing room in the kitchen area was where the dancers and drag artists got ready. That door was locked because they kept their things in there. It was safe back there, so if someone rode their bike to work, they kept it in that big dressing room, too."

Mercury recalled. "Sometimes, when I was there with my male dance troupe, the Rockets, they would have porn stars there too. When Jeff Stryker was appearing, he got our dressing room. We had to get dressed in the kitchen. We joked that we were getting ready using the pots and pans as mirrors."

"The entrance to the kitchen area was across from where the doorman sat outside the back bar. There was not much else back there—just the kitchen, the offices, a couple of pay phones, and the entrance to the back bar. If somebody was looking around back there, that doorman would ask them what they were doing. The doorman was there to enforce the leather or Levi code at the back bar. Women could go in the back bar if they obeyed the dress code." Patrykus remembers breaking through the wall to create what was to become the back bar. "There was a brick wall that opened into that back bar area, which was actually the garage area of the Bijou."

To publicize the opening of the new space, Carol's held a contest to name the back bar. Apparently, there were either few entries or folks just decided there was nothing more fitting than the Back Bar. The official opening of the Back Bar was delayed due to the blizzard of January 1979, when Chicago was hit with an estimated 18.5-21" of snow over two days.

Carol's Speakeasy, 1355 N. Wells St., is running a "Name the Back Bar Contest" now through April 20.

The Back Bar, "Name the Bar" contest from Gay Chicago, *ca. 1979.*

The back bar had two 19" TV screen monitors, which primarily showed *Colt* physique slides or images from *Drummer Magazine.* Eventually, porn sometimes played in the back bar.

"The back bar at Carol's had a very different atmosphere from all the other bars in the place," offered Arthur Johnston. "That bar felt more like it belonged at the Gold Coast than at a dance bar. I worked at that back bar for probably six months or so." After half a year at the back bar, Johnston moved to the dance bar.

When Dan Neniskis went to Carol's, he usually made his way directly to the back bar. "The back bar at Carol's was no Gold Coast or Redoubt (65 W. Illinois St.), but it was cruisy, and I was always on the hunt."

Ray Thomas shared, "Out of all the bars, I think Carol's Speakeasy was the first one that had a back room that I remember. I remember I went in there twice, and it was like, 'It's too dark. I can't see who's touching me. I've got to get out of here.'" (de la Croix. 'Chicago Whispers #68,' *Chicago Outlines*).

"All of Carol's was dark," said Paul Mikos. "But the back bar, where the porn was playing, was even darker."

Given the back bar's different vibe, it was only fitting that the music there was different as well. The back bar at Carol's had a jukebox that offered a mix of country and hard-driving rock with a four-on-the-floor beat: Cheap Trick, Foreigner, Bruce Springsteen, Foghat, the Eagles, Supertramp, REO Speedwagon, and Bob Seger.

"Once I was at Carol's with a friend," shared Greg McFall, "At closing, I was standing there talking to Mother Carol and trying to find my friend. All of a sudden, my friend came out of the backroom buck naked except for a pair of cowboy boots, shouting for someone to turn the lights on in the back because he couldn't find his clothes."

Alvin recalled, "That bar was kind of raunchy to me. They used to have sex in the backrooms... It's always amazed me that so-called predominantly white bars can get away with doing stuff like that, whereas the Black bars couldn't..." (de la Croix, 'Chicago Whispers #124,' *Blackines*).

"After cops raided the back bar, it wasn't as dark back there anymore," added Chuck P Kass. "And by the mid to late 1980s, the bar was discouraging messing around at all in the backroom."

"There was never butt sex back there. Maybe a hand job, but more likely just some feeling up. Not a full blowjob, maybe just a taste," added Malone Sizelove.

"I loved the Carol's back area with the porn movies playing or the slides," said David D. "I always wanted to go sit on the risers in that back bar and have sex or watch sex or just feel the erotic potential around me. No one talked much in there. Everyone seemed to be waiting for someone else to make a move. That room usually had that kind of sexual tension."

"In the back right hand corner of that room," shared Del B, "was a darker area where some sex went on. I think for a while they also had a tire swing back in the back bar when they redid it once to give it the feeling of someone's garage or backyard."

"The back bar was quieter," said David Plomin. "If you connected with someone on the dance floor, that was where you went for a drink afterward. If they were interested, they would come along—if not, they would stay on the dance floor."

Robert Kimmons saw his first porn movie in the back room at Carol's. "It was *Winner Takes All* (1983) from Falcon Studios. I found out the name later. I remember it specifically because it starred my favorite gay porn crush, Lee Ryder (1959-1991)."

The first night he went to Carol's, Kimmons stood outside for a while, mustering the courage to enter. "I was 19. I said to the doorman. 'I'm not sure I'm old enough to be in here,' and he replied, 'You look to me like you're old enough to do whatever you want—now get the hell in here.'

"From the moment I turned that corner into the main bar, I knew I was in the right place. I moved to the side of the dance floor and stood there, trying to take it all in. Then the music changed, and there were cheers and a swell of people behind me moving to the dance floor. I literally got swept up and taken to the dance floor as 'So Many Men, So Little Time' came on. I ended up in the arms of a short, hairy bodybuilder who pushed against me and started gyrating his hips as the song washed over us. He leaned in and asked if it was my first time there. I said it was my coming-out night. He smiled and said, 'And you're all mine.' He was amazing."

Kimmons also recalled a Carol's summer party in the dead of winter. "I was dancing with a doctor, so he had the real amyl nitrates. I was sober at the time, but on relapse. I was dancing with a brandy snifter full of Rum 151, a cigarette, and my Zippo lighter. The doctor was dancing with a bottle of poppers and turned suddenly. I was doused with poppers and rum as I was lighting my cigarette. When I struck my Zippo the rum and poppers made all these blue flames that died out quickly. Rather than be excited in the least, everyone who saw the flash of fire thought it was part of the floorshow. They applauded and kept dancing. People saw everything there. The wildest things could happen and the Carol's crowd wouldn't bat an eye."

Although gay nightlife and a good number of gay people had moved to the North Halsted Street and Lakeview area, many gay men did not mind the walk home from Carol's in Old Town. Some men walked to get some fresh air and sober up a little. Other guys walked to save a few bucks. And many men walked because they were looking for action. Walking home through Lincoln Park, many chose a route further to the east, along the lagoon and the Lincoln Park bushes—an extremely active outdoor sex area for gay men.

Frank Nichter reminisced about his late night walks home from Carol's. "After the bars closed until dawn, from the lagoon to Diversey and west of the lagoon, there were men there. There used to be so many bushes on that hill, like the Rambles in New York... Walking home from Carol's at night there would be so many people there. As I recall, it was sex on site. It all happened right there. On the top of that rise by the statue were trails as well and those were probably the most active."

"My place looked down upon the Lincoln Park bushes," said David Roy Cohea who lived in a high rise at 2470 N. Clark. "The bushes were the busiest along the lagoon north of there. In the early 1970s, that was free sex in the pre-AIDS era. Cruising was sporadic during the day, but once the bars closed the bushes would be flooded with guys looking for someone. The cops raided the bushes with their sneak attacks just like they did at the Belmont Rocks. The police drove right up to the bushes with their lights off, then jumped right in and started looking for arrests."

"After the bars closed they would be so fucking busy," recalled David D. "The bushes were a cultural thing for me at the time, like so many gay men. I had become so repressed by the culture in the day that at night we turned into these sex hunters. The bushes down along the lagoon were a known sex area. Going there at 2 a.m. or 3 a.m. was a little dangerous, but that danger fed the adrenaline and it fed the sexual high. Guys were having sex all over in there."

In 1982, *Drummer Magazine* #38 covered the Chicago nightlife scene and Carol's received a sizable chunk of copy. "The ads say, 'Where Chicago parties and Chicago says, 'You're damned right!' Carrying on the honored tradition of the late Chicago legend whose name it still bears, Carol's Speakeasy is unquestionably the city's wildest and most popular disco/party bar.

"The place is almost cavernous—four separate bars, the one in the back being a magnet for leather (and somewhat removed from the music), a huge dance floor, unobtrusive table-seating areas—all of it pulsating under Chicago's most incredible sound system.

"And no one in Chicago can throw a special party like Carol's can. From the sublime (like a recent reception for players in the National Invitational Volleyball Tournament) to the unthinkable ('Drugs for Drags' needs no comment), Carol's parties invariably attract the largest cross-section of Chicago's gays—with the leather turning out hot and heavy on weekends (especially late)."

Artist durkART captured the feel of the era and a Carol's Speakeasy evening by printing this memory across his Carol's ID. "...1980, as you walked towards the disco, you would hear the bass of the music getting louder as you walked closer and closer. Finally, you could hear the song being played as you swung open the old wooden door, turned to your right, and walked 6 or 7 steps. You had to present your membership card, and the doorman would let you in. Overlooking the dance area, you were greeted by multi-colored hues of flashing lights, music, people dancing, the fogginess of secondhand smoke encasing the surroundings, and, of course, all the smiles...and as the giant disco ball slowly rotated, again casting a twinkle in your eye and thinking to yourself, 'tonight's going to be another magical night.'"

Though he preferred the back bar, when Dan Neniskis was in the main room at Carol's he liked to sit by one of the big bass speakers. "I liked to sit there and feel my clothes vibrating from the sound."

Ed Z was intimidated when he first went to Carol's. "I had not been to many bars, and it was full of nice-looking men. I started going there more. I would go there looking for a hook-up—sometimes I was successful and sometimes not, but I had fun. Carol's was cruisy, but it was also a party bar. We used to love to go dance on those big pedestal speakers that they had for go-go boys."

"There were speakers flanking the dance floor, and dancers would be on those," recalled Brian D Smith. "One of the speakers was against the far-left wall by the end of the front bar. Beside it were stairs that went to the basement. They stored the beer down there. I had sex on those stairs a few times."

"And the guys with the fans," added Daniel L. "I liked watching those too. Those fans were big on the dance floor, especially at Carol's."

"The energy was so intense, all those shirtless men!" said Doug Barnes. "I probably first went there around 1981. I had been a DJ down in Champagne at theBar for years." TheBar was a popular gay club that was open for decades at 63 Chester Street in Champagne, IL. "Sometimes, my friends and I would take a field trip. When we drove up, we had a ritual. As soon as we turned a bend and could see the Chicago skyline in the distance, we would fire up the joints or drop acid or whatever, so by the time we came into town, we were ready to party. Once, I got the chance to be a guest DJ at Carol's for an hour. The DJ was a friend, and he let me spin. You got to the booth by climbing a wooden ladder attached to the wall by that front bar. Going up that ladder you came through a hole in the floor of the DJ booth. The booth was above the front bar with a great view of the dance floor."

Terence Alan Smith, aka Joan Jett Blakk, loved to go dancing at Carol's. "I loved it! Loved it! Loved it! The main songs I think of when I remember dancing there were 'Got to Give It Up' by Marvin Gaye, 'Love Hangover' by Diana Ross, 'Vertigo/Relight My Fire' by Dan Hartman, 'Do You Wanna Get Funky With Me?' by Peter Brown, and 'Funky Sensation' by Gwen McRae."

John Barak was a punk and New Wave music fan but added that Carol's was still the place to be even though he wasn't a disco fan. "I was more into Pet Shop Boys and New Order, Billy Idol, New Wave. I used to tip the DJ to play my music. The best was having them play Iggy Pop or, better yet, 'Dancing with Myself' by Billy Idol. I wore combat boots to dance, and I would be pogoing with myself in a mirror." Pogo is a punk dance of jumping with legs and feet together, as though on a pogo stick.

"There was nothing like being at Carol's—screaming and swinging to Sylvester," recalled Michael Harrington. "I met my first lover there. I was there with some friends, and Gary was there with his friends, and we were all on opposite sides of the room. Looking across, our eyes connected, and I went over and asked him to dance. We danced for 30 solid minutes. We were covered in sweat by the time we came back to where we were standing. That was when I realized that Gary's friends were deaf and that Gary was deaf as well. When I had asked him to dance, he had been reading my lips. That was the first night of our relationship that lasted six years."

In 1979, the bar had a tribute to Elvis Presley on the two-year anniversary of his death. Elvis Evening included drink specials, Elvis lookalikes, assorted performances, prizes and giveaways, and, of course, plenty of Elvis music. A decade later, the bar had a similar evening on the anniversary of the death of the queer dance superstar Sylvester (1947-1988) with music videos, live footage, and non-stop Sylvester.

"The highlight of Carol's was meeting my partner, Jeff, in the back room," said Chuck P Kass. "He came up to me and started talking and gave me his business card...and the rest is history. We were together for 35 years."

Diana McKay worked all over town from 1971 to 1995, including Carol's Speakeasy. "Once, I was performing 'The Boss' at Carol's. I was on top of one of those large speakers, and I spun around and fell right off the speaker and onto my tailbone. That floor was hard! But I spun around, got up, and started dancing. I acted like I had practiced falling off the speaker the entire time. Another time at Carol's I came in off the street with a big group of friends. David Boyer was at the door, and he pointed to the wall where they posted upcoming events at the bar. I was scheduled to perform that night! I had completely forgotten and showed up with no gown, no wig, nothing but a group of friends. David said not to worry about it, 'Just go in with your friends and party in the room.'"

Making Carol's the place to be required ongoing work. Changing the décor was one way to keep the Speakeasy experience fresh. Carol's went through transformations several times a year. The new interior began with a general theme. The staff then worked to bring the concept to life. Turning the enormous space into something new and making the metamorphosis "something that you just have to see" was no minor task.

"Dan Gould was our set designer most of the time," said Allen Patrykus. "He would direct everything and tell us where to paint, what to do, and what to make. We did all our own decorating and work. The themes would change pretty often. It was a lot of work. Sometimes, we would still be painting on the day of the party. With the high Carol's ceiling, the quality of what we made was less important because we were able to do a lot with lighting and effects. Music and lighting were so important for creating atmosphere there."

Billed in the press as "a return to the decadence," the Roman Toga Party at Carol's included a showing of the film *Caligula* (1979), the Bob Guccione produced film about the depraved reign of the Roman Emperor. The feature received an X-rating despite a cast that included Helen Mirren, Malcolm McDowell, and Peter O'Toole. Also playing at the Roman Toga Party that year was the 1981 Bijou XXX feature, *Centurians of Rome*, showing in "the imperial dungeon." *Centurians of Rome* was a gay XXX feature set during the reign of Caligula. The tagline of the movie was—'Caligula's Empire...Ruled by Passion! Destroyed by Lust!' On promotional fliers for the Roman Toga Party, the street address of Carol's was done in Roman numerals—MCCCLV N. Wells.

Joey McDonald remembers the toga party. "I remember how crazy things became. The back room was very busy that night."

TL Noble is a gay disco lighting and design genius. His work helped define the era by creating the atmosphere of several huge Chicago gay clubs—the Bistro (420 N. Dearborn St.), Paradise (2848 N. Broadway), and Bistro Too (5015 N. Clark St.), to name a few. After the closing of Paradise in 1986 and prior to the opening of Bistro Too in 1987, Noble did some work at Carol's Speakeasy. "When Paradise closed, David Boyer snatched me up to come to Carol's and be his lighting guy. I fixed a lot of things when I was there. I installed a large pyramid of mirrors that rotated, and I created some new effects with the lighting.

"That Halloween, we had a TV space show theme. We did a tribute to several big television shows that were set in space. We had each one in a different place in the bar. The main stage was the bridge from *Star Trek,* complete with sliding doors. In the back, we covered the pool table with a tarp and added a cardboard frame. Then, we wrapped the base with Mylar, painted cardboard window frames, and put Plexiglas on it. In the end, it looked just like the Land Rover from *Lost in Space.* We did something else from *Battlestar Galactica.* The costume contest was on the main stage. Since that was made to be like the bridge of the Enterprise, for the costume contest, the doors would open, and the contestants would appear." That evening, there were prizes in several categories—Best Overall Costume, Best Drag, Sexiest Costume, Group or Couple's Costume, and a Space Queen Award. Noble added, "Halloween costume contests were a big deal in those days. People had fun but they took it very seriously. Some timed it so they could go from bar to bar and compete for cash if their costume was good enough."

David Boyer added, "We had a $1000 cash prize, and we would have 200-300 people entering the costume contest. For Halloween, we always had a theme. One year, the décor was tied into the first Batman movie, so the bar was transformed into a Gotham-themed Halloween complete with a bat cave."

Some years, Carol's offered added incentives to make it the place to be on Halloween. One year, Carol's offered poppers. "The first 300 patrons in the door for Halloween at Carol's this year will receive a free bottle of Hardwood 'liquid aroma.'"

Boyer recalled one Halloween when the theme was the Phantom of the Disco, "... The dance floor had a balcony around it, and we had the crashing chandelier. We changed the back area and made it into the catacombs of Paris."

Themes for the bar often coincided with the release of a new movie, which sometimes included a screening of the film. In 1978, Supermania came to Carol's in preparation for the release of the *Superman* movie starring Christopher Reeve. All those who came to Carol's that night wearing a 'Metropolis character costume' kicked off the party with a free cocktail. Later in the evening, there was a Superman as well as a Lois Lane lookalike contest, along with prizes for the 20 most notable Metropolis citizens. Someone arrived at the party as a piece of kryptonite. For many, a room of sexy Supermen in speedos and nerdy dudes in horn-rimmed glasses ready to rip open their shirts were reason enough to attend.

Promotional advertisements for the *Mommie Dearest* party featured Allen Patrykus in a jockstrap and leather vest. He is on his hands and knees on the dance floor with a number of wire hangers strewn around him. "And Miss Regina is over me in boots and stilettos and with a can of Comet cleanser flying. Miss Regina's dialogue bubble says, 'Scrub that dance floor, bitch!'"

Carol's also had a Boogie in Bedrock bash, with the Speakeasy receiving a Stone Age makeover to become a *Flintstones* world. Stone homes. Boulder-mobiles. Dinosaurs galore. The works. The 'Yabba-dabba-doo time' festivities included a costume contest with prizes for the best Fred, Barney, Wilma, and Betty. In keeping with the theme of the popular adult animated series (1960-1966), ribs and "brontosaurus burgers" were served that evening.

David Boyer recalled the décor overhaul that coincided with the release of *Raiders of the Lost Ark*. "We went to Fertile Delta plant store and bought every plant they had and brought it back to the bar. So, at the entrance to Carol's, it looked as though you were going through a jungle. That time, we also had an idol statue that shot flames."

In 1985, Thunderdome was the theme, accompanying the release of the new Mel Gibson and Tina Turner film *Mad Max Beyond Thunderdome*. There were no survivors. "We had dancers in cages with spiked shoulder pads," said Boyer. "We had a pen of live hogs in the bar. During the set up, they got loose and shit and pissed everywhere."

Chuck C Kass remembers Thunderdome as his favorite. "The best part was they put the big dome over the dance floor!"

"On Halloween, my friends and I always did drag," said Johno. "One year, we did Showgirls from Beneath the Thunderdome. Another year, we took first place in Felicia's (aka Jim Flint) Halloween Ball at Park West as the Solid White Tuna Supremes. After we won, we paraded our costumes around town. We went down to Wells St. to Carol's Speakeasy. After that, we went trick or treating in our costumes to the Over 21 Bookstore (1347 N. Wells St.). The guys behind the desk gave us each a bottle of poppers to put in our purses."

Carol's was known for parties and happenings of every sort, from a Masquerade Ball to hosting Mr. Mid America Leather. Sex was always a popular event theme at the Speakeasy. Carol's had full-on lights-out parties with the bar handing out flashlights.

"The Hotter N' Hell parties gave out dog tags," recalled Allen Patrykus: "There was one dog tag for the Erection Party, then the next party would have a different dog tag with the name of the party. Some people collected them all on a chain."

Peter Lewicki was the DJ at the Erection Party. Promotions included a dress code—worker clothes and flashlights. The theme was construction. Those in construction clothes and hard hats got in for free.

"Inside the bar, we had enormous tools hanging from the ceiling. Saws, wrenches, screwdrivers, hammers—those giant tools were constructed out of cardboard and aluminum foil," explained Patrykus, "But with the high ceiling at Carol's and the right lighting...you couldn't tell."

Ron Helizon reported in *Gay Life* that the Erection Party was "a man's party for all you machos, jocks, and those that just like to watch them." Performers for the evening included Chicago Molly, Diana McKay, and Amanda Winters.

Amanda Winters had been a cast member at the Baton Show Lounge (436 N. Clark St.) and performed at several venues around town. She eventually moved to the West Coast with dreams of becoming an actress. On Jan. 3, 1981, the small plane carrying Winters and four others crashed on the return flight to Long Beach after a trip to Vegas.

Some parties at the Speakeasy were about politics and current events. Divorce isn't often a reason for jubilant celebration, but the 1980 Carol's Speakeasy Pride Parade float had an orange color scheme to coincide with the pending divorce of rampant homophobe Anita Bryant from her husband Bob Green. The divorce had been announced the month before. After the parade, there was an Anita Divorce Extravaganza at the bar. Hostess for the evening was Tillie the Dirty Old Lady.

Bryant (1940-2024) and her manager/husband Bob Green (1931-2012) parlayed Bryant's fame as a former Miss Oklahoma into a gig as the singing spokesperson for Florida orange juice. Bryant then used her modest fame as a juice peddler to attack an ordinance in Dade County, FL. that extended basic civil rights protections to homosexuals. Bryant fanned public hysteria at the notion of gay teachers with cries that children would be molested and/or converted. Due to her outcry and her Save the Children campaign, Bryant helped to overturn the anti-discriminatory measure.

In the 1970s, gay people started to feel part of a larger gay community. The gay press connected us by reporting on the injustices faced by LGBT people nationwide. Broadened awareness brought a sense of kinship. This expanded view of community was evident in the aftermath of the 1973 Up Stairs Lounge arson fire in New Orleans that killed 32 bar patrons. LGBT folks across the country had grieved the tragedy—offering assistance and raising funds.

In 1977, the Anita Bryant and Bob Green driven attacks on the rights of gay people in Dade Country Florida got plenty of coverage in the gay papers. An attack on gay people in Florida became an assault on gay people everywhere.

On June 14th 1977, Bryant was scheduled for a Flag Day performance at Medinah Temple (600 N. Wabash), and Chicago's gay community was not having it. Shuttles ran from the gay bars to the demonstration. 5,000 protestors turned out to show how they really felt about Bryant's agenda of hate with posters such as—"Anita Preys for Us, Pray for HER," "Anita and the Klan Go Hand in Hand," "Save Our Children, From Anita," "Equal Rights for Gays," and "Who is She?" In addition to a successful protest, Chicago gays held the Orange Ball, actually a couple of them. The Orange Balls were large-scale fundraisers that raised thousands to battle Bryant's homophobic measures in Florida. In addition to the Dade County show of homophobia, Bryant and Green also founded the Anita Bryant Ministries to "work with homosexuals to change their lifestyles." Enough said.

So three years later, in May of 1980, when news broke that the deeply Christian marriage was now deep in the toilet, the gay community found it ample reason to celebrate. Orange was the theme of the Anita Divorce party at Carol's, which included a performance of Tammy Wynette's 'D-I-V-O-R-C-E' with some wicked new lyrics.

One of the many causes that the Speakeasy supported was the annual holiday Toys for Tots drive by the gay motorcycle club, the Chicago Knights. The Knights group began in 1971 as a break-off group from the Second City Motorcycle Club, founded in 1963. By the 1970s, there were half a dozen gay men's motorcycle clubs in Chicago.

Local gay entrepreneur Jim Flint was elected president of the Chicago Knights in 1976. Flint's bars at the time included the Baton Show Lounge and the leather bar, the Redoubt. Extremely popular in the community, Flint was a force on more than the bar scene. Among other things, Flint was influential in local politics and in the gay Chicago sports leagues. He also founded the Continental Pageantry System in 1980. Jim Flint made things happen. With Flint in charge of the Knights, the annual Toys for Tots donation increased every year. The campaign was in synch with the Knights bylaws, which stated that the club was to, "conduct projects of a public service or charitable nature to benefit legitimate charities and to promote the good image of the Club."

In 1982, the Chicago Knights collection for Tots for Tots made the news, and not in a good way. "In 1982, the [Toys for Tots] benefit raised $22,000 for various charities, including the Salvation Army. The Knights received media coverage that year after the Salvation Army refused its $1,400 donation because of the nature of the gay club. The Salvation Army claimed the decision was in 'harmony with our philosophy,' and the anti-gay nature of the organization has been under scrutiny ever since." (Franco, Baim, 'Salvation Army defends anti-gay bias.' *Windy City Times*, Dec 7, 2011).

In the article, Harley McMillen (d. 2013) is also quoted about the 1982 incident from an interview he gave in 2000. "We did try to give money to the Salvation Army and they refused it because of who we were. We got quite a bit of publicity over that. Even Mike Royko (1932-1997) wrote about it in one of his [*Chicago Sun-Times*] columns, in terms of 'why wouldn't they take the money, and what about the people that need help?' The general public opinion was very much in our favor. Since then I have never given the Salvation Army a dollar, but that's just my personal thing."

Carol's was a popular collection spot for Toys for Tots. Dan Neniskis, from the Knights, recalled one evening that he was shaking his change jar at Carol's for Toys for Tots. "They let us stand inside in the area between the coat check and the bar. I was in full Chicago Knights regalia—grey police shirt, tie, Sam Browne belt, military dress slacks with the white stripe, and black leather Muir cycle cap. I was standing there with one of those bar-size olive jars. I was shaking the jar, saying, 'Nickel, dime, penny, quarter.' People were really giving up their change that night. The olive jar was getting fuller and heavier. I was shaking it to get more donations, and all of a sudden, the bottom of the jar broke. There was glass and change everywhere, and right as you came into the bar. We scrambled to pick it all up as best we could."

"The coat check was where you bought your drugs at Carol's," said Frank Nichter. "Hand your coat over with the cash and get the MDA with your check ticket. Very clever and unnoticeable."

The incomparable Miss Regina in the Carol's Speakeasy store, photo courtesy of Allen Patrykus.

Miss Regina was a popular coat check person. "Miss Regina always had John, her dog, with her on a leash when you saw her out," recalled Chuck P Kass. "In the late 1970s and early 1980s, you saw them all around. Regina was heavily into drugs. Once, a bunch of us went to an after-hours party in a loft building, and Miss Regina went too. She did not have John with her for some reason. Anyway, we were going up to the party in a freight elevator, and Miss Regina was so stoned that when the elevator doors opened, she collapsed on the floor. People just stepped over her to get out of the elevator and go into the party."

Mark Hultmark added, "Miss Regina was crazy, but we loved her."

Past the coat check was the seating area to the side of the dance floor, which was designed like a park. From there, you could either go two steps down to the dance floor or one step down to the front bar. Beyond the front bar was Carol's store, a retail area that sold chips and munchies, poppers, T-shirts, headbands, active wear, cock rings, bandanas, and lube. Hand fans were popular at Carol's store, but poppers were the top-selling item week after week.

"Ida Guevarra, who had been with Mother Carol for years, ran the Carol's retail area," explained Allen Patrykus. "To access the gift shop Ida went through a locked door in the women's john and into the back of the store. Ida would be sitting at the counter of the gift shop, and I'd say, 'Hey Ida, what's going on?' And Ida would say, 'I am so fucking high.' But she would be sitting there completely motionless and never messy—you would never know she was high to look at her."

Arthur Johnston laughed, "Drug use was different then. Sometimes, you would come into work, and someone would put shot glasses on the bar filled with different pills. Quaaludes were big. But there were a lot of different things in all colors and sizes."

Handkerchiefs were a popular item at the Carol's store. The hanky code was still a common way for gay men to communicate sexual preference, position, or kink. The hanky color denotes the activity. Dark Blue = Anal, Light Blue = Oral, Gray = Bondage, Yellow = Water Sports, etc. Placement of the hanky in the right or left rear pocket indicates active and passive partner in the activity—the left side being the active partner, and the right side being the receptive. The hanky code was still a popular means of conveying preference for hooking up, but by then hankies in a gay dance club had another use. Aunt Ethyl had come to town.

"Carol's was the first place I saw people dancing with an ethyl rag in their mouths," recalled Chris G.

For a high on the dance floor some patrons soaked the knotted end of a hanky or bandana with ethyl chloride and danced with the knot between their teeth with the other end of the rag dangling from their mouth. Ethyl could be purchased from onsite dealers in many gay clubs at the time for around $10-$15 a bottle.

As a popular dance club, Carol's Speakeasy also hosted several musical acts. Most were well attended and often the place was filled to the rafters. Queer underground film superstar turned dance diva, Divine (1945-1988), came to Carol's to do a few songs from his dance album, *Jungle*

Jezebel. The ads read, "See that Jungle Jezebel, Divine singing the hits 'Native Love' and 'The Name Game.' When Divine appeared at Carol's, the show promptly sold out.

Hi-NRG singer and out and proud gay heartthrob Paul Parker performed at Carol's Speakeasy in 1982. Parker's catchy club hit 'Right on Target' and the follow-up single, 'Shot in the Night,' were from his debut album, *Too Much To Dream.* Parker's LP was produced by legendary queer record producer Patrick Cowley (1950-1982).

Chuck P Kass went to the Paul Parker show, "He was so handsome, and he put on a great show. Dancing, strobes, poppers, and tambourines—what more can I say?"

Those who came to see Dead or Alive, featuring lead singer Pete Burns (1959-2016), recalled Carol's as being packed that night with the drink line three or four deep the entire evening. The dynamic dance duo, the Weather Girls (Martha Wash and the late Izora Armstead), also appeared on the Carol's stage. When they performed their dance anthem, 'It's Raining Men,' the place went wild.

Dance and R&B vocalist Linda Clifford headlined at Carol's on more than one occasion and always drew a crowd. The disco diva's string of dance hits included 'Runaway Love,' 'Don't Give It Up,' and 'If My Friends Could See Me Now.' The late vocalist Vicki Sue Robinson (1954-2000) best known for her enormous 1976 disco hit, 'Turn the Beat Around' was at the Speakeasy. The British pop singer Limahl performed there as well. His real name is Christopher Hamill—Limahl was an anagram of his surname. In 1984, he had an enormous hit with the title song from the film, *The NeverEnding Story.*

The Chesterfield Kings, Dena Kaye, and Wacker Drive also performed at Carol's.

Chicago-born disco singer Loleatta Holloway (1946-2011), who scored huge dance hits with 'Love Sensation,' 'Dreamin,' and 'Crash Goes Love,' commanded the stage at Carol's. "The event was not terribly well attended, but she put on a great show," added Grant Smith of her 1982 appearance. Smith recorded Holloway performing 'Love Sensation' at Carol's. The uploaded footage is on YouTube.

Sharon Redd (1945-1992) had a show at Carol's as well. Redd was a club singer who had several solo dance hits, including 'Can You Handle

It' and 'Beat the Street.' Prior to embarking on her solo career, Redd was a member of Bette Midler's backup trio, the Harlettes, from 1972-1978. Redd died of complications from AIDS at age 46.

Claudja Barry, a top dance singer with hits that included 'Sweet Dynamite,' '(Boogie Woogie) Dancin' Shoes,' and 'I Will Follow Him,' had a listening party for her biggest single, 'Down and Counting' at Carol's.

Disco and hi-NRG favorite Pamala Stanley ('Coming Out of Hiding,' 'If Looks Could Kill,' 'I Don't Want to Talk About It') graced the Carol's stage as well. "Fans loved her," shared TL Noble. "She was one of the few acts who liked having dance remixes of their songs playing while they entertained. She was smart. During the long musical segments, she twirled these colorful hand fans (called 'fanning'). The crowd loved it."

Carol's Speakeasy hosted Viola Wills (1939-2009) who had hits with disco covers of several popular tunes including 'If You Could Read My Mind,' 'Up on the Roof,' and 'Stormy Weather.' Ava Cherry came to the Speakeasy to promote her debut album, *Ava Cherry—Ripe*. Cherry was David Bowie's backup singer, muse, and girlfriend from 1974 through 1978.

Jeffrey Pool remarked, "All the acts there were great, but to me, the most impressive performer at Carol's was Brenda K. Starr. Her voice was so intense and perfect that it gave me goose bumps." Starr had just released her debut album, *I Want Your Love*, and the lead single, 'Pickin' Up the Pieces,' was becoming a huge dance hit.

The British synth-pop trio Bronski Beat came to Carol's in 1989. General admission tickets were $10. The April Fools Day Show started at 1 a.m. Bronski Beat was a unique act at the time. All three members of the British synth-pop band (Jimmy Somerville, Steve Bronski, and Larry Steinbachet) identified as gay. Not only that, but the band wrote and performed songs about gay life. Their string of dance hits included 'Smalltown Boy,' 'Hit That Perfect Beat,' 'Why?' and 'Ain't Necessarily So.' Steinbachet died in 2016, and Bronski in 2021.

Dean Ogren recalled the evening, "Bronski Beat was a late show. The place was mobbed. When they got on the stage, the place just went up for grabs. People went nuts. Bronski Beat was incredible."

Bartender Jeffrey Pool was working his usual spot at the front bar the night of the Bronski Beat show. "And all I was doing was working. Nights like that, you're there, but you're getting drinks and that night it was just person after person after person. So, I appreciated the money, but I couldn't really appreciate the Bronski Beat show when it was going on."

In addition to being a venue for a wide array of musical acts, Carol's hosted meet and greets with gay porn stars. The appearance of gay porn stars at Carol's was made easier given the proximity of the gay adult theater, the Bijou, two doors south. Al Parker, Peter Berlin, Rex Chandler, Jeff Stryker, Justin Cade, Blade Thompson, and Rick Donovan were only a few of the adult performers who appeared at Carol's to sign photos and meet fans. A porn star or two in the house was something more to offer, something more for people to talk about, and another thing that made Carol's Speakeasy the place to be.

Grant Smith recalled when Peter Berlin came to Carol's in 1983. "That was a big deal for me. We cruised each other, but that was it, and that was enough. He was all about the cruise anyway."

Gay adult film star, Rex Chandler (center), posing for photos at Carol's Speakeasy, photo courtesy of Gay Chicago Magazine.

"I have a picture of me with Jeff Stryker in front of his limo when he was at Carol's," said bartender Jeffrey Pool.

Jeff Stryker was the biggest gay porn star of the era. He came onto the gay XXX scene in 1986 with a string of XXX hits that included *Powertool* (1986), *Bigger Than Life* (1986), *Stryker Force* (1987), and *In Hot Pursuit (1987)*. Stryker appeared at Carol's Speakeasy several times over the years to sign photos, videos, and even dildos for fans.

Paul Mikos has a Polaroid of Jeff Stryker nibbling his ear at Carol's. "I have no idea why, but he asked me to dance. So, we did, and the crowd kind of formed a circle around us. I was so embarrassed."

"The porn stars I met at Carol's were mostly polite and quiet," recalled David F. "I remember meeting Lee Ryder there as well as Rick Donovan. I also met Lance (1962-1991) from *Leo & Lance* (1983)."

"We had porn stars there quite a bit," recalled David Boyer, adding that Carol's was even the site of porn events, like the premiere of *Dynastud*, a 1986 gay adult feature and a parody of the nighttime soap, *Dynasty*. The XXX version involved the doings of the Harrington Boys of Beverly Hills. "That drew quite a crowd. The cast was there, and everyone just sat on the dance floor and watched the movie. Then, they had pictures signed by the cast." The *Dynastud* cast included Christopher Lane, Melchor, JD Slater, and Rick 'Humongous' Donovan.

In April 1991, the Speakeasy was the site of the premiere of the gay porn movie *Bedtime Stories* from Catalina Video. The film starred former Mr. Carol's Speakeasy, Ted Matthews, in his film debut. The cast included Chad Knight and the late Johnny Rahm (1965-2004). The film was marketed as, "an all night tale of all male hard-pounding action." The premiere included an autographing session, video giveaways, free posters, and more.

Jaime Krohn remembered Carol's as being a filming location as well. "A bunch of us were asked to be extras in a comedy movie called *Datenight*. I'm not sure if it was a gay movie or not, but based on the extras..."

Datenight was not a gay movie. The film starred the comedy duo of Al Franken & Tom Davis (1952-2012). Shot in Chicago over the months of April and May of 1985, *Datenight* includes a big scene at Carol's Speakeasy. The film was released on VHS under the title *One More Saturday Night*. The Internet Movie Database sums it up as "a comedy about datenight antics." The cast included several Chicago actors, Meshach Taylor, prior to fame on *Designing Women*, and John Cameron Mitchell, playwright and future star of *Hedwig and the Angry Inch*, as Teenager #2.

Legacy of Lies, a TV movie released in 1992 that starred Michael Ontkean, Eli Wallach, Patricia Clarkson, and Martin Landau, was also filmed at Carol's Speakeasy. "They had the bar at their disposal for a couple days," explained David Boyer. "Martin Landau filmed in my office. In those scenes, you can see the pictures on the walls of the acts the bar hosted—drag queens, porn stars. They didn't bother to change the wall pictures. That movie also has a scene where a guy runs down the alley by the Over 21 Bookstore and the Glory Hole."

Allen Patrykus typically worked at the dance bar in Carol's. "That was the bar off the dance floor with the lampposts and the rounded end. We called it the dance bar because that's where the male dancers were. Two dancers were usually on the main stage, and one would be at the dance bar, and they would rotate. At the dance bar, we usually had three bartenders and three bar backs. [There were] three cash registers.

"The guys would dance between the two light poles; each of those light poles had five glass globes, four on each side and one in the middle. The lampposts weren't dance poles. Those globes were real glass, and if they got knocked off, they would shatter. The dance stage was slightly lower than the rest of the bar. There was a cubbyhole underneath it; that's where I kept my backpack and tips. I had one coffee can for change and one coffee can for bills. I remember when my tip jar was full, trying to empty it into my tip cans without folks seeing, even though I was exposed to people on almost every side. Then, at the end of the night, the bar bought back our quarters, so it took a while to get out of there.

"Something I loved about being a bartender," added Patrykus, "was when a regular or someone who was coming to my bar that night—when I would see them coming my way. Although I was always busy, I made it a game to have their drink ready by the time they got to the bar.

Sometimes, when I did, they would just empty their pockets of all their extra change—and that could be a lot of money.

Male dancer at Carol's, author's collection.

"When we counted out our money at the end of the night, they let the bar cat, Trash, out of the back. He would hop up on the bar and come say hello to all the bartenders while we were rolling our quarters and counting our tips. Trash was a feral cat. I believe Roger (Hickey) found him, got Trash all his shots, and brought him to the bar. His litter box was in the back in an outer room of the offices. Trash didn't have food bowls. No one fed him, but we all gave him treats. Mostly Trash was a mouser. He killed all the mice and rats in the place, so after we cleared out the money and left the bar and before the office staff and cleaning crew came in, Trash had free run of the place and that cat never went hungry. Trash was a good mouser and became the bar mascot. After we got raided in 1985, we didn't see Trash for days. The cops were smashing things in there. Trash was probably petrified. Who knows where he hid and watched from?"

Jimmy Doyle recalled when his boyfriend danced at Carol's' "I used to love to go and watch him dance. Guys would tip him, and I thought it was so hot. You know, desire him and keep giving him money, but he is going home with me."

Mercury danced at Carol's for a while. "The dance bar at Carol's always reminded me of Donna Summer because it had a lamppost, so it always made me think of 'Bad Girls.'"

"I was mesmerized by one of the Carol's dancers," offered Robert. "He was this blonde guy, naturally muscular, and he would come out with only a bandana and only dance with that, but he would never expose himself."

David Boyer added that when the stripper troupe Hunter and the Headliners performed at Carol's, they worked on the main stage and then in the crowd. "They would dance wherever they could for tips."

Beyond the dance bar was a pool table and a few pinball and video games. The wall behind the game area had three painted murals of Mother Carol's mouth. "The flipper pinball machines were in the alcove between the front bar and the Carol's store," explained Patrykus. "In the back were the joystick and video games—Pacman was huge, Space Invaders, Centipede. That got to be a big thing to do at Carol's as well. There would be drinks and quarters lined up. Challengers waited for their chance at all those games. Some guys got calluses from the joysticks."

Brian D Smith liked to shoot pool at Carol's, "There were two pool tables in the back. I learned to play pool at a lesbian bar in Lansing, Michigan, so I liked coming to Carol's and being able to hold the table for four or five games. That was a kick."

Pizza Night at Carol's often meant drink specials and a sexy crowd-pleasing event like a Best Buns or Hot Chest or Hairy Ass or Wet Underwear contest. Amateur skin contests, cocktails, and free pizza were a surefire way to bring in a crowd. At Carol's, Michael K was frequently the emcee for such evenings.

Michael K (Kucharski) began as an informal protégé of Mother Carol. The gravel-voiced bar personality and emcee was a natural before a crowd. As a host, Michael K could be relied upon to lift the energy of the room. He worked at numerous Chicago gay bars and emceed dozens of events and fundraisers over the years. Michael K was voted "Top Male Bar Personality of 1980" by the gay community. *Gay Life* columnist Jon-Henri Damski joked that Michael K had a resume that read—"every bar, everywhere."

Nightlight personality Michael K., photo courtesy of Gay Chicago.

"At Carol's Speakeasy, Michael K would sit at my bar all evening and drink Coca-Cola," said Allen Patrykus. "Michael and Ida were roommates. They had a huge storefront apartment and would throw a big Christmas party every year for all the gay bar people. Bartenders, bar owners, entertainers—huge parties with enormous meals they would make. Michael K was always Santa and he would pass out the gifts, which were usually tiny packages of drugs, at least mine always were."

Diana McKay shared the stage with Michael K and Mother Carol at Carol in Exile and performed at the space after Michael K took over and it became Broadway Kunfusion. "Michael K was so wonderful to me," said McKay. "He gave me encouragement to keep me going. He made sure I was working. He was a big emcee and knew everyone. He advised me about things. Michael K was a mentor when I needed one."

One high-profile hosting gig at the bar was the Mr. Carol's contest, which always drew a packed house. Mr. Carol's was a sought after title—competition could be fierce. Carol's Speakeasy was an extremely popular bar, so representing Carol's in the Mr. Windy City competition came with a certain amount of clout and a built-in cheering section.

To register for the Mr. Carol's contest, entrants were required to answer the five questions on the registration form and sign at the bottom. The questions were—What's your name? Where do you live? How old are you? What's your sign? What are your hobbies?

The Mr. Carol's title came with cash, prizes, and free cocktails for life. Mr. Windy City came with more of the same. The contest was originally a beauty, body, and personality contest—Mr. Windy City represented the modern "out" gay man, who also happened to have a great body and face.

Finalists in the Mr. Carol's Speakeasy contest, with the winner moving on to the Mr. Windy City event. In 1975, Mother Carol cofounded the annual contest that ended in 1992, photo from the author's collection.

As AIDS gripped the community, the contest became more politically charged and the title was a platform. Paul Adams (1954-2000) was a Mr. Carol's and went on to become Mr. Windy City in 1987. In 1993, Adams reflected on bringing a political consciousness to the title. "Even though it was this beauty contest, I found after I won that people actually paid attention to you. It seemed funny at the time because the contest had nothing to do with politics aside from doing benefits and showing up here and there to lend a name to something. [The contest] prompted me to take a stand...

"The politics came after the first March on Washington in 1987. Well, actually, it was joining the pre-ACT-UP Chicago group, CFAR (Chicago for AIDS Rights). That group was what really got me interested in politics—the politics of AIDS and the politics of lesbian and gay rights because those were the issues the group was trying to address." (Keehnen Interview, 1993.)

Wrestling at Carol's with bartender Jeffrey Pool (left). Wrestling Night at Carol's was also the setting for one of the last big Chicago gay bar raids in 1985, photo courtesy of Jeffrey Pool.

Another popular event at Carol's was wrestling. Thursday evenings meant a few matches before dancing. A spread of mats covered half the dance floor. The weekly matches led to Jeffrey Pool getting a job at Carol's. "I was student teaching in Buffalo Grove as a wrestling coach. Carol's had wrestling nights where you could win $25. I kept coming back and winning—bartenders, the bouncers, all their biggest guys, I beat them all. Finally, David Boyer said to me, 'If you can bartend half as good as you wrestle, you have yourself a job.' I said I could, but I didn't know how to bartend. I was a young and innocent wrestler. That front bar, right as you came through the door, was usually mine."

Wrestling Night at Carol's was the setting of one of the last and most brutal of Chicago's gay bar raids. Raids on Chicago gay bars hadn't been an issue for a while. Many gay people thought we had moved beyond all this, but in September of 1985, Carol's was raided once again. The raid was the work of the Metropolitan Enforcement Group, aka MEG, aided by Chicago Police. Neither group honored the legal rights of patrons or employees.

Reporter Tracy Baim covered the raid for *Gay Life*. "Members of the Windy City Wrestling Club were on the mats when over a dozen men came through the front and back doors, guns pointed and flashlights shining.

"Approximately 15 officers entered the bar around 11 p.m. Besides a possible customer or two shouting that the police were there, no one heard the men announce that they were police officers. Instantly, patrons and employees were forced to lie face down on the floor, some for more than an hour. According to witnesses, when bar patrons would ask what was going on or made attempts to get up, they were kicked back down.

"Some patrons said the officers wore rubber gloves, including when frisking people, though no strip searches or cavity searches were conducted.

"One by one, each person in the bar was told to answer detailed questions about their lives, such as their jobs, their mothers' names and addresses, if they were married or were they ever married, where they live, and other questions." (Baim, 'Drug Raid at Carol's.' *Gay Life*, Sept. 19, 1985).

Allen Patrykus was there. "They came through the front yelling with their guns drawn, and at the same time, they came through the back. The backdoor alarm had been turned off to give the police access. We are fairly sure who it was. They used to work at Carol's and had been in jail. At the time, they were doing some painting at the bar. They were in trouble with the law, and we figured they probably made a deal. When the cops came through the door, I wasn't even on duty. I was waiting to go on. It was clear they had been casing the place. I wasn't behind the bar, but when they came in, they pointed to me and said, 'He works here.' Then they pointed to someone else who just happened to be there and said, 'He's a bartender too.'"

Mark Hultmark was the DJ on the night of the raid. "A cop came to the DJ booth and told me to stop the music. They made me come down, and they gathered us all up."

Patrykus added, "When the lights turned up, and the DJ cut the sound, it was silent in there, and this big cop yells, 'Okay, fellas, where are the guns?' I remember thinking, 'this is a gay dance bar—we don't have guns.' No one had a gun."

"They yelled for us to lie down on the dance floor," recalled Brian D Smith. "Many of us were shirtless. It was scary. I was high and drunk, and it scared the shit out of me. I was there probably two hours. We weren't allowed to enter or leave or get up, even to go to the bathroom. They were being real dicks about it."

Jeffrey Pool added, "And they used those batons like cattle prods and said stuff like, 'You like it.' Making fun of people."

The *Gay Life* coverage continued, "According to sources, some MEG officers constantly threatened people, saying they would send them to the hospital. Several people were called names such as 'cocksucker' and 'faggot.'

"The manager of Carol's that night, David Boyer, said he is positive his rights were not read until after he was questioned. He said no one ever showed him a badge or announced what they were in the bar for. Initially, he and others in the bar thought they were being robbed. Close to 1 a.m., the officers cleared out.

"Boyer, who had given the keys over to the officers, said extensive damage was done to the bar, including the breaking of locks and rummaging through files. In addition, the bar membership files were gone through, and money from the register was left lying around during the entire raid.

"Sometime after the bar raid, one of Carol's bartenders, Fred S, was arrested in his home. He was charged with two counts of delivery of a controlled substance—MDA, which is a form of speed, and one count of possession, again of MDA. Early Friday morning, Fred's roommate, Andrew D, in trying to bail Fred out, was arrested.

"The arrests at Carol's were: Donald P, on two counts of delivery of MDA and one count of MDA possession; Michael T, charged with one count of obstruction of police."

Boyer was further quoted as saying, "The way we were treated, with rubber gloves, and other things, it made me feel like not quite a real human being—between the verbal and physical abuse. ...At one point, one cop asked if it was okay to piss at the bar; another said 'No.'" (Baim, 'Drug Raid at Carol's.' *Gay Life,* Sept. 19, 1985).

The late Richard Bubel (1937-2019) wrote of his experience, "While watching live wrestling: the sound of running feet and the glare of bright lights shining into the bar. I turned towards the door and was met with a gun and light in my face. The order, 'Hit the floor and put your face into it or you'll get it busted.' I was pushed to the floor and kept there for approximately 45 minutes. Guns were brandished, and the constant threat of physical harm was given. I was kicked in the side when I lifted my head to see what was going on.

"I was searched, and my wallet was taken. My ID cards were copied onto a form and such questions as to relatives' names and addresses, property owned, and clubs I might belong to were asked under the threat of harm if I did not answer.

"A form was given to me, and I was told to read and sign it. I explained that in the poor light and without my reading glasses, this was impossible. I was told to, 'Sign it or else.' I was walked to the front door, and my picture was taken ...

"At no time until I was at the front door [leaving] did anyone identify themselves as a police officer; verbally, badge, or ID card.

"The above is what happened to me; there were approximately 50 people in the bar, and to my knowledge, similar tactics were used on all."

Allen Patrykus stated, "I was on the ground for maybe a half hour when a cop came over, kicked me, and said, 'You're next.' Meaning that I was next to be processed. There were two processing stations—one on the display case of the Carol's store and the other at the coat check. When we were processed, we were made to remove all contents from our pockets and wallets. That was all photographed. The man who went through my belongings was asking for the names and addresses of my parents and brothers and sisters, my employers, past and present, and past and present residences. Noting all the answers on a form. Then he told me to read and initial line by line a form and sign it at the bottom. With all the hitting and yelling going on, there was no doubt I was not being given any choice in the matter. He then told me to go to the front door and get my picture taken. I saw that all my belongings were strewn about, and I asked him if I could get them, and he let me do so. My picture was then taken at the front doors." Patrykus was then told to leave the premises. "We couldn't even wait outside, so most of us who worked at Carol's congregated down the street at the Glory Hole."

Patrykus and Bubel filed a lawsuit. "We were the only two who gave our real names. Before we decided to sue, we waited a few days. We needed to check with our day jobs. First, we had to tell them that we were gay, and then that this horrible thing had happened to us. Even after we did that, we took about three weeks to get up the nerve to call the ACLU. When Harvey Grossman came on the phone, he said, 'We've been waiting for someone to say something.' It was Richard and I and a third, a Joe Doe. The rest were class action suits."

In the *Chicago Tribune*, William B Crawford Jr. reported that members of the Northeastern Metropolitan Enforcement Group [MEG] and four Chicago police officers were sued for a million dollars. The suit alleged that 16 MEG officers entered the bar without proper warrants, ordered patrons to lie on the floor, forced them to fill out forms disclosing detailed information about their personal lives, photographed them, and made only one arrest.

In the *Tribune* story, Illinois legal director of the ACLU, Harvey Grossman, is quoted as saying. 'This is one of the most massive violations of civil rights we have seen in Chicago in the last decade...What the agents did was to take the occasion of serving an arrest warrant on the bartender and turn it into a raid on all who were present at the time." (Crawford, 'Suit Assails 1985 Raid on Gay Bar.' *Chicago Tribune*, Dec. 16, 1986).

Patrykus added, "We wanted three things—money paid to the 52 people who were there, a public apology in the newspapers, and the return of all the photographed wallet contents. We ended up getting it all. We had $5,000 awarded to the 50-plus people who were there, as well as $10,000 for Richard and me. After that, we had an unmarked cop car sitting outside our home for years."

In the aftermath, queer columnist Jon-Henri Damski wrote, "Freedom is a heavy drug—but it is not a controlled substance. You cannot control people and have a free society. You cannot stomp on the pleasure realities of people and have a free society. ...These gay bar raids in Chicago are out of control. With guns, you can control 50 people for an hour—sure—but that's hostage justice, not American justice. ...Real justice is, as Plato said, 'minding your own business.' People and pleasures differ. Now is the time to cool the raids and let different people mind their own business in the pursuit of their own pleasures."

After the raid, Brian D Smith was uneasy going out to bars for several weeks. "After I was held there, I was anxious. I was apprehensive about going out for a while. I still went out, but my solution to that was to get at least a couple cocktails in me fast because then I didn't give a shit."

"Briefly, there was talk about the bar suing for damages," added Patrykus. "But I don't recall the bar doing anything. I think in the end, it was mostly an attitude of, let's just get past this."

Almost 40 years after covering the raid, publisher Tracy Baim reflected on the incident. "This was among the last of the big-city, big-gay bar raids. It was high profile and a bit odd because of who was doing the raid. Regardless of that, though, it was seen as just another form of harassment of a gay bar at a time when Chicago's gay community was fast gaining clout in our city council and the mayor's office. The community finally was strong enough to start confronting these kinds of raids with both internal and external support, and it was a turning point. We were no longer easy targets for law enforcement."

As a community, we were coming into our own, and Carol's was a bar rooted in community. Arthur Johnston summed it up by saying, "Carol's was a bar that gave back."

The Speakeasy supported many LGBT organizations through donations, hosting benefits, and allowing non-profits to collect at the door. The bar hosted occasional talks and community meetings. Carol's invited local politicians to discuss their stance on issues of interest to the gay community. Only a few years prior, the thought of a politician intentionally appearing at a gay bar was inconceivable, but in Chicago, the gay community had become a voting bloc worth courting.

The *Chicago Tribune* reported on March 12, 1980, "...At the request of [gay entrepreneur] Chuck Renslow, a Kennedy delegate from the 9th District and prominent gay businessman, Ted's nephew, 22-year-old Michael (RFK's son), and his 20-year-old daughter Kara campaigned Saturday night at five gay establishments. The two, accompanied by Secret Service men, went to the Bistro, Gold Coast, Sunday's (430 N. Clark St.), Carol's Speakeasy, and the Baton (where they stayed to watch the female impersonators' show). If their schedule allows, they'll make the same rounds again this weekend." (Aaron Gold, 'Tower Ticker' column. *Chicago Tribune*, March 11, 1980).

"Carol's Speakeasy was very good about hosting fundraisers—Horizons, the Rodde Center, and a lot of different gay organizations," added Rick Karlin. "One night, at a benefit for the Illinois Gay and Lesbian Task Force, they had karaoke. I didn't want to do it, but they insisted. So, I did 'Don't Cry for Me Argentina' as Mayor Jane Byrne because, at the time, she was supposedly living in Cabrini Green to show the housing was safe. So, I sang, 'Don't Cry for Me in Cabrini, the truth is I never lived there. In an apartment filled with roaches, I kept my promise, it didn't snow here.'"

Jane Byrne became Mayor of Chicago in 1979 by following a surprise victory over sitting Mayor Michael A. Bilandic, in the Democratic primary. In the campaign, Byrne criticized Bilandic's snow removal record and policies. Byrne surprised everyone when she was elected Mayor of Chicago, coming into the office on a wave of what were referred to as "snow protest votes."

Welcome to Oz week at Carol's meant a dramatic transformation into the magical Land of Oz. To kick off Oz week, there was a costume contest not only on Friday night but on Saturday and Sunday as well. Folks went all out with their costumes. Some wore a different elaborate costume each night.

At midnight on Friday, the Speakeasy hosted a performance of the short musical *The Wizard of A.I.D.S.: Aware Individuals Deserving Survival*. The musical was intended to entertain and educate, especially young people, about the importance of practicing safe sex. Condoms and safe sex information were distributed to the audience as part of the performance. Rubbers have a big role in The *Wizard of A.I.D.S.* Spoiler alert—at the show's climax the Wicked Witch of Unsafe Sex is suffocated by an enormous condom. *The Wizard of A.I.D.S.* was the creation of actor, writer, director, and producer Michael Barto (1962-1995). Barto wrote the musical in 1987 after learning he was HIV+. He moved to Chicago shortly after. Barto died of AIDS in 1995 at age 33.

Saturday during Welcome to Oz week had an Oz costume contest and some surprise performances on stage. At Carol's that night, there was also seasoned man candy on display—the men from *Daddy Magazine*.

The educational HIV musical, the Wizard of A.I.D.S., was performed on stage at Carol's Speakeasy, photo courtesy of Lee Newell.

The appearance of the *Daddy* men had a tagline that tied it to the Oz theme. "All the scarecrow, the tin man, and the cowardly lion needed was a good daddy."

The Sunday Oz festivities featured "Christmas in Kansas" square dancing with a caller and featured performances by Dena Kaye at 8 p.m. and 10 p.m. Country dancing had become an enormous hit at Carol's. Thursdays went from wrestling to Country Western Night.

Country Western Dancing at Carol's, photo courtesy of Lee Newell.

"Country and line dancing was very popular in other places, and I was a big fan of country music," said David Boyer. "So we decided to have Country Two-Step Night on Thursdays. All we needed to get it going were a country DJ and someone to teach the dance steps. We hired a DJ from Atlanta and had him come in, but the dance instructor fell through.

Fortunately, a cowboy named John had just moved into town, and he started teaching two-step lessons. Eventually, it became so popular that we started the Chicago Original Country Dance at Carol's on Sunday afternoons. Sometimes, there would be 500 people country dancing—gay men, lesbians, and straight couples... We had the space for it."

Carl R went to both Thursday and Sunday country dancing at Carol's. "For me, country night wasn't about sex or getting lucky. I felt lucky every time I went there. When I left Carol's, I was tired and happy after three hours of dancing. It was exercise. It was physical contact. It was camaraderie, and it was such a good time. David Boyer hosted. Two-stepping and line dancing were a great way to meet people and see them regularly. An entire cadre went there every week.

"I loved teaching newbies to dance. I wasn't some big stud, but being a good dancer gave me the confidence to ask guys to dance. I didn't care what people thought seeing me dance with this hot guy or that hot guy. If people thought anything about it, I hope it was, 'that Carl was sure smart to learn how to two-step so well.'

"I taught my ex-boyfriend and his new boyfriend how to two-step. My ex was a born leader for two-step, so I showed his new lover, Helmut, how to follow. I thought they would be great, but it was a disaster—my ex was not leading, and Helmut was not following. After they were done, I asked my ex what happened, and he looked at his big Austrian boyfriend and said, 'Do you really think I am going to lead with him?'

"My favorite dance on Country Night was shadow dancing. That was so sexy. Shadow Dancing is a slow two-step, the follower turns, and the leader is holding them from behind and doing the same steps, crotch to butt cheeks. Shadow Dancing was sexual, sensual, romantic, and the leader is holding the follower so closely that their cheeks are touching."

Brian D Smith came for country dancing every Sunday. "Ready to boot, scoot, and boogie. That was by far my favorite night at Carol's. I met so many people there. I love a country waltz, and I especially like to spin at warp speed, keeping my eye on my partner so the rest of the room fades away and I don't get dizzy. My friend Sammy and I used to do that. Sometimes, we would fast spin for the entire song."

"I am turned on by cowboys and love seeing men in jeans and flannel, cowboy boots, and cowboy hats," said Phil Bernal. "I was young, and it was so easy to pick guys up, and if a guy is good on the dance floor, he is usually good in bed. Country night brought in an enormous crowd. My usual way to pick up guys was to stand by the side of the dance floor, and when guys came off the dance floor, I would say something like, 'I would have loved to join you out there, but I don't know how.' Then he would say something like, 'Let me teach you,' and then I might say something like, 'Well, I'm better at the horizontal bop.'"

Country Night, photo courtesy of Lee Newell.

The group that showed up for country dancing was typically a friendly, regular crowd. Seasoned dancers were mostly helpful with the novice two-steppers, and Cowboy John was on hand for lessons. Country night continued for years at Carol's. I Am a Carol's Cowboy buttons became an accessory. Country night prompted many Carol's

Cowboys to shop for western wear—boots, hats, shirts, vests, the works. Conditions were perfect for onsite fashion shows. The enormous boot and clothing store Alcala Western Wear (1733 W. Chicago Ave.) supplied the fashions for more than one runway show at Carol's..

Square Dancing at Carols, photo courtesy Lee Newell.

In 1987, Country night at Carol's was the birthplace of the Chicago LGBT square-dancing club, the Chi-Town Squares. The Chicago LGBT Hall of Fame reports that Jerry Cohen (1943-1991) and DJ Ron Goldman were the founders of the group. David Boyer was aware of interest in forming a gay square-dancing club and discussed it with Carol's DJ Goldman. Notices were placed in the gay papers announcing the formation of the club. Almost 30 folks showed up for the first meeting. Eventually, the Chi-Town Squares even fostered subgroups such as the She-Devils, a troupe of mostly bearded square dancers in drag.

Steve Marton remembers Country Night. "My friends and I would go on these marathon evenings back in 1984. I was 23 at the time. We would go to Exit (1653 N. Wells), Berlin (954 W. Belmont), the Loading Zone (46 E. Oak), and Cheeks (2730 N. Clark). ... But those nights usually started at Carol's. We would go to the back leather bar there and get a dime of MDA. Then we each ordered vodka and grapefruit, which we had to down in 45 seconds. Then, we got a second drink, and we would go sit on the cruising ledge along the wall and watch the parade. Carol's was our launching pad for the night. We went there on country night and would be very high on MDA. We would trip out watching the line dancing. The men were so into it and knew all the moves—all in cowboy drag with their mustaches and jeans with cowboy hats and boots. It was completely hot."

Marton adds, "MDA made me more outgoing, more smiley, and much more fun. MDA was basically this onset of warmth, love, and good feeling. It heightens sensitivity to sound, so it was great for listening to music. Colors were also great, so sitting on that 10-12" ledge and watching it all while tripping was something."

"When you went to Carol's," said Lori Cannon. "You had to watch where you parked and be mindful walking to and from your car. The best places to park were the side streets off Wells and LaSalle. Parking on the side streets was free. To save extra cash, many of us stowed our coats in our cars and ran through the cold to get inside, hoping there wouldn't be a line at the door when we got there."

"Parking was not great around there," recalled Dan Neniskis. "Once I drove my ragtop jeep there and came out, and my car had been broken into and whoever did it stole my radio."

John Barak was mugged twice near Carol's. "Once, I was thrown to the ground and had a knife put to my neck. They took everything I had on me, including my gold chain. The other time, I was parked across the street. My friends and I came outside to have a smoke, and when we did, this guy came out of the Bijou and hit that little step, and his knees wobbled, and he fell. We were wasted, so we started laughing. As we were standing there, a guy ran by wearing my jacket. He'd just broken into my car. I started chasing him, but he was playing cat and mouse. He was keeping far enough ahead that I would keep chasing him. In a couple of minutes, I had no idea where I was, and I got mugged. He led me into a trap, and I got my ass kicked."

Inside the bar, Carol's management went to great lengths to keep theft to a minimum. "There was a security crew of 13 with four at the front door, one at the door to the leather bar, one to the side of the dance bar, and floaters on duty to watch for thefts or spot fights. It was a huge space to monitor," said Allen Patrykus, "but it needed to be done."

Dean Ogren had a life-changing experience at Carol's. "In 1980, there was a raffle, and one of the prizes was a package ticket for IML (International Mr. Leather). The guy I was with won the ticket, but he didn't want it, so I went. That changed everything. That free package ticket to IML was what began my involvement with the leather community." Ogren also recalled the IML Victory Parties at Carol's when free access was allowed between Carol's and the Bijou.

Carol's had notable IML-affiliated parties in 1989, 1990, and 1991. Jeffrey Pool recalls those IML weekends at Carol's as "one nonstop party. There was a law that they had to clear the bar so that we would get everyone out of Carol's and through those double metal doors outside or into the Bijou, and once we cleared the bar, we let everyone back in."

"I wasn't big into drugs and alcohol," said Richard F. "And Carol's was too much of a party bar for me. I did go there for an IML party. After the contest at the Vic Theater (3145 N. Sheffield), there was a party at Carol's. I was there dancing in my harness. Then, the bar closed at 4 a.m., but a door opened in the back so we could go upstairs to the Bijou and continue the party there. I grabbed a guy who was there by the harness and pulled him upstairs. We ended up dating for a while... It didn't go anywhere, but it started with that great 'let's go fuck' moment."

"When we drove up from St. Louis, we would go to Carol's," recalled Rick Garcia. "I loved the place. We had nothing like it in St. Louis. We had dive bars and a pretty glass and chrome bar, but we didn't have anything like this. We liked the atmosphere and clientele. It felt homey, comfortable, and very welcoming. People just had fun there. This was a big city disco. Grittier. The guys were hotter, the music was great, and the atmosphere was completely exhilarating. Carol's just captured the excitement of being gay at that time."

Tay went to Carol's on New Year's Eve of 1984. "My mentor had a wonderful dinner for a few close friends with live lobsters flown in. As part of this elaborate dinner, we had MDA—as we called it, Mary, Don't Ask—in our dessert coffee. Then we went to Carol's. One friend didn't even make it inside. He went to the Over 21 Bookstore and stayed there all night. So, five of us went to Carol's. I was into New Wave and punk and a complete music snob about it, but that night, I learned to appreciate old disco in a new way. I was dancing like crazy to every song.

I remember hearing 'Shame' by Evelyn Champaign King and the blend and sound was so infectious that it broadened my appreciation of dance music. 'It's Raining Men' by the Weather Girls and 'Let the Music Play' by Shannon were a couple more songs I remember dancing to that night."

"I was living in the suburbs," said Ed Z, "So I had to be careful not to drink too much. Some nights, I even took LSD so I could drink more. Then, instead of driving home, I would take a cab to Man's Country."

"Friday night was a $3 door charge and cheap drinks. So, there were a lot of drunks there on Friday nights, lots of guys looking for dick," said Allen Patrykus. "Saturdays tended to be more about groups having fun. That was the night for bringing straight friends to the bar and parents. Saturdays, there were more women."

"Our busiest nights were Friday and Saturday," offered David Boyer. "Every Friday, the place would be packed. And Mondays—that was quarter drink night."

Ads for the Monday Special read, 'Fight inflation, Drink at Carol's!'

"We called the quarter drink nights, drink-and-drown nights," said Bob M. "When we were going for quarter drink night, we would say we were spending the night at DD's. It was just something between me and my friends, most of whom I met at Carol's."

Lori Cannon was a Friday night Carol's gal. "Joseph LoPresti and I had a standing date to meet and go dancing there, but Joseph rarely danced with a partner. We would start off dancing together, and then he would move on. Everyone was mesmerized by Joseph's beauty."

Rail added, "Everyone wanted to dance with Joseph LoPresti."

Joseph LoPresti also danced at the Bistro and Coconuts. In 1980, LoPresti was dancing at the Bistro when he was named *Blueboy* magazine's Man of the Year. He later danced at Berlin and was a DJ at Cell Block (3702 N. Halsted). LoPresti eventually moved to Miami. He died in South Beach in 2014.

"If you wanted to party and have a good time, Carol's was where you went," said Bruno Mondello. "I remember dancing to Sylvester and 'I Feel Love' by Donna Summer on poppers and being on the dance floor and guys fan dancing, which was really cool to watch. I remember all of it. The art of cruising was important at Carol's, too. That bar was how it was done."

Shane K described cruising as, "The hunt for casual sex, often using nonverbal communication. The first step is eye contact, often prolonged and repeated. That is followed by one or more parties discreetly grabbing or rubbing their own crotch to indicate further sexual interest, though sometimes the crotch grab is followed by eye contact."

"Carol's was built for it," said Paul Mikos. "There was a ledge along the wall past the front bar and dance floor where people would lean and socialize and cruise. That was my place in the early 1980s—it had none of the pretensions of the Bistro or lines outside. I lived about two minutes from there at 1503 N. Clark, so I was always dragging guys down the side streets and alleys back to my place. I'd go back and forth on weekends."

Ad copy. "Whatever your type—you'll find him at Carol's."

"Carol's was a bar for people who really liked to dance," said David D. "I went there with a woman friend. We loved it and became regulars. Once, we were invited somewhere upstairs for a VIP after-party of some sort. The party was very dark, and people started having sex—men, women, everyone all over the place. I lost track of her. I was on the floor blowing some guy, and I looked over, and she was on the floor next to me making out with a gay guy. We both turned our heads and caught sight of each other and exchanged this look of, 'Can you believe we are doing this?'

"When I went there, I was a fashion student. I used to wear these geometric men's pieces and dance. I used to think I was so cool as a fashion artist bringing my fashion there. And when I danced, I did this thing where I would dance and then freeze. So I thought I was bringing this new dance there, too. When I see myself doing this now, I shake my head and think, 'tragic.'"

"I broke up with my boyfriend there," recalled Pat Batt. "We'd been together a while. We moved to Chicago together. We had been having problems for a while, and one night at Carol's, I was standing there watching him dance, and the song 'I Will Survive' came on. It was just one moment when I thought to myself, 'you know what? I will survive.'"

"Once this guy broke a date with me," said Daniel L. "And a couple hours later, I saw him dancing with some twink at Carol's. I was such a brat. I thought, 'No one does this to me.' I ordered a rum and coke and waited until he got in line for a drink, and I got in line behind him. Then I poured my rum and coke over his head and stormed out. He had no idea what had happened. He slugged the guy behind him. The police got called, but no charges were filed. I didn't go to Carol's much after that."

Rick Karlin had a dance routine he did there with his friend Calvin Harris, aka Miss Peaches. "We had a certain signal that when I danced away and reached back to smooth my hair, I would fall back, and Peaches would lift and throw me, and we would land in a 'ta-dah' pose—then start dancing again. We had so much fun just being silly.

"Everyone did poppers at Carol's. I would put an unlit cigarette in a poppers bottle and sniff the cigarette filter. That worked great until some guy leaned over and tried to light my cigarette, and the whole thing went up in flames."

"We would go back and forth between Carol's and then maybe the Glory Hole or pop in the Over 21 for a blowjob and back to Carol's," offered Terence Alan Smith aka Joan Jett Blakk. "The next morning, five or six of us would all meet for breakfast to rehash the night before. We went to the pancake place at Broadway and Belmont, which we called the Casa del Pankiki. After breakfast, we would go to the Belmont Rocks. That was how we spent a lot of our weekends. We went out a lot. Everyone did. I never had a bad time at Carol's. I remember one night being on one of those big speakers dancing to 'There Before the Grace of God' and looking out over the fabulous and diverse crowd, and it felt like the whole world was working out. I was up there dancing with a friend who I had a crush on for years, and we started making out. We went to the back bar and played around a little more. Later that night, I wore his boyfriend's harness."

Jean recalled the era and herself at the time, "I was a punk rock lesbian monster. Drinking was my social scene. All my friends were gay guys and we went to Carol's. We were restaurant people, and it was a late bar. We went after the restaurant closed, so not until 1 a.m. or 2 a.m."

"Everyone was living their best life on Carol's dance floor," added Dean Ogren. "It was a place to forget your troubles, be fabulous, and have a great time. It was all so perfect and wonderful, and then that whole world caved in."

In 1995, the late Carol's owner, Roger Hickey, reflected on first hearing about what was to become the AIDS epidemic, "...I was working at Carol's on weekends, during the days in the office, and there was a lot of discussion...about all the people who were coming down with this illness...That's when it was called GRID (Gay Related Immune Deficiency)."

Ad with Carol's streetlamp logo.

Hickey explained that initially, there was talk of poppers being the source of the disease and having discussions about not selling them anymore. "...That was when I first became aware of it (GRID/AIDS)," continued Hickey. "...Over a very short period of time, it seemed like it took on a life of its own. ...In addition to a sense of dread, there was almost a sense of panic. Everybody's aware that there's this thing out there killing people in our community, but nobody was sure what it was.

It was a pretty scary time, a very scary time. It seemed to cast a pall over the entire community.

"As a result, nightlife rapidly began to change. In particular, in a club like Carol's, everything was so open and spontaneous and careless and carefree. ...People didn't go out, and the people that did go out didn't party like they used to. It seemed like the community grew old over a very short period of time. It was an entirely different attitude and a different feeling." Hickey added that, eventually, the panic began to subside. "It was probably...late '89, '90 before it seemed to work itself out, and people started realizing that, you know, life does go on...People started coming back, and although it never hit its peak of what it was in 1978 or '79, where you'd have a thousand people in there every night of the week... [After a few years] you would see 1000 or 1500 people in there on a Friday night or a Saturday night. By then, the street had changed. The action moved up to Halsted Street." (Jack Rinella Interviews, 1995).

Ironically, Hickey later became a prime force in anchoring North Halsted as a gay nightlife and retail enclave. Hickey became co-owner of the popular nightspot the North End (3733 N. Halsted) as well as the owner of the Cell Block for a decade. Hickey died in 2012 at age 76.

The entryway at Carol's Speakeasy, as with many gay bars and businesses of the time, served as an unofficial LGBT newsstand with all the free Chicago gay papers—*Gay Life, Gay Chicago, Babble, Windy City Times, Chicago Outlines*, etc. The Carol's entryway was also an information center—a place for community notices, fliers for stage productions, benefits, and shows. There was member information and brochures for numerous LGBT organizations—Dignity Chicago, the Lincoln Park Lagooners, IMPACT, the National Gay and Lesbian Task Force, Horizons, New Town Alano Club, Gerber Hart Library, the NewTown Writers, the Rodde Center, Black/White Men Together, Queer Nation, GLAAD (Gays and Lesbians against Defamation), the Frontrunners, the Smelts, the Chi-Town Squares, the Chicago Gay Men's Chorus, and more.

With HIV attacking Chicago's gay population, the number of emerging AIDS organizations was staggering. Many of these were grassroots operations, arising out of desperate need and peopled by volunteers. AIDS organizations needed funds and a way to get their message out. The necessity of places like the Carol's entryway as avenues of information cannot be overemphasized. A few AIDS organizations that had information in the Carol's entryway included AIDS Care Chicago, Open Hand Chicago, the Names Project, AIDS Legal Council, AIDS Foundation Chicago, Bonaventure House, ACT UP Chicago, AIDS Walk Chicago, the Kupona Network, AIDS Pastoral Care Network, Chicago House, Test Positive Aware Network, and Howard Brown. The entryway at Carol's was also a site for the distribution of safe sex materials and free condoms. A bowl of condoms was kept filled, courtesy of the Reimer Foundation.

Founded in 1991, the Reimer Foundation served a key role in the community during the worst years of the AIDS epidemic. The Reimer Foundation provided free condoms, which were distributed at dozens of Chicago area bars, bathhouses, and LGBT affiliated offices and businesses. The Reimer Foundation also produced safer sex promotional cards and posters.

As the epidemic worsened, gay bars, in general, expanded their service role, becoming the sites of countless fundraisers and collections for various AIDS research and service organizations. Carol's hosted AIDS benefits of every sort—raffles, giveaways, food drives, benefit performances, pie tosses, and auctions. Bachelor Auction Night helped to raise money to pay the expenses for people with AIDS (PWAs) who wished to attend the 1987 March on Washington. There was Casino Night at Carol's, with the bar transformed into a Vegas casino. The proceeds from the evening were distributed to several AIDS organizations.

"The way I explain AIDS to younger people is to say think of the room we are all in," said Terence Alan Smith. "Now imagine it half full. That was how powerfully AIDS hit. I had to get involved. We all did. We all had to get it done because no help was coming. Quarantine before care was the way things were being done. We also had to carry on with our lives while having this all going on. It made us stronger, and we went through that together. Something I loved about Carol's was that although all that was going on, it was a place of so much fun in spite of everything—that is something I cherish from that time. At Carol's, you knew you would have a good time despite anything that was going on outside those walls."

"When I was in school in Iowa City, sometimes we made road trips to Chicago," said Boomer. "Carol's was always the first place that we would stop after that four-hour road trip. We didn't even drop off our clothes. We went right from the car to Carol's. We would get there later on a Friday, around 10:30. Walking into Carol's, the thing that struck me was the people. Not the individuals so much as the amount of people. When we walked in, the front of the bar was so broad, so wide that you suddenly saw this mass of people dancing, talking, coming and going. The atmosphere was exuberant. This was around 1987 and 1988, and AIDS was everywhere. It was becoming a part of everyone's world, even in Iowa City. Carol's was important. It was a place where a lot of people could sort of put all that aside for an evening and have a good time."

"The best nights at Carol's were when I went with my friends," said John Barak. "About six of us would go, and we always had fun. Carol's was our regular place on Wednesdays. Mondays were Alfie's (900 N. Rush) because Pepe was the DJ and he spun New Wave. Tuesday was Broadway Limited with quarter drinks. Wednesday was Carol's. I can't remember why, but we were there every Wednesday. And then Thursday was the Bistro. That was our weekday bar party schedule."

"From 1988 to 1991, about ten to twenty of us newly sober guys would go to Carol's to dance and for camaraderie and fellowship," said Frank Nichter. "The bar was big enough where we could congregate in a certain area and have fun. The bar was very accepting of us. It was exciting and safe to go there together, and we always had a great time."

Terry Gaskins first went to Carol's in 1985. "I had just come out. I came here from Macomb for a visit. I only knew one or two gay people in the world. Going to Carol's, there was a whole dance club full of gay people, and even though it was mostly gay men, it was confirmation that I was where I should be. I was a hot mess that night. Poppers. Dancing. Living. After that weekend, I was at the Amtrak station making plans to move to Chicago at the end of the school year. And I did. I came here with my camera bag, two milk crates of records, a turntable, a tiny TV, and some clothes."

"In its day, there was nothing quite like the community that existed in that space," added Steve Migalski. "Carol's was a party bar, but it was also about freedom and the profound magnitude of exuberance that comes with it. Every time I went there, the place was full of joy, merriment, and camaraderie."

There was no denying the increasing migration of gay nightlife to the Lakeview and North Halsted area. Carol's was a cab ride away, but still doing great business on weekends. The end of the Speakeasy came in an unexpected and horrific way.

"Jeffrey Dahmer sat at my bar when he came into Carol's," said Jeffrey Pool. "He liked the same spot. At the very end of the bar, as you came in the door—the very first seat in the bar. Always ordered a light beer and didn't talk much to anyone that I saw."

"He was at my bar the night he left with Jeremy," said Allen Patrykus. "He was right in front of where I washed the glasses. He ordered three or four bottles of Michelob, and then it got busy. I didn't see him until the end of the night. Jeremy, who was a friend of the bar, came out of the back when we were counting our money, and he was with this guy. Jeremy was wasted and said he was leaving. Tim, who worked at Carol's and was Jeremy's roommate, said, 'Girl, you are not going to Milwaukee.' They went back and forth for a while. Meanwhile, Dahmer is just standing there, not saying a word. We didn't think Jeremy was going, but we were counting our money and getting out of the bar, so there was a lot going on. The next day, Tim called me. He couldn't find Jeremy, but his wallet was there. So, we went to the police, and that didn't amount to much more than them implying that it was just another flighty queen who went off someplace."

In addition to being a friend of the bar and a pal to several on staff, Jeremiah (Jeremy) Weinberger worked two doors north at Bijou Video Sales at 1363 N. Wells. Mike Donner worked there as well. "That was the Bijou offices. The bottom floor was shipping and receiving. The offices were on the second and third floors. Steven Toushin lived up there. There was also an attic that was sometimes used for video shoots. Mostly films were shot on location somewhere else, but sometimes scenes were shot upstairs at the offices.

"We were a family—Ralph was a production assistant, customer service, and jack of all trades. Candy from Tennessee did customer service. Teddy was in customer service. Lonnie was the manager of the theater. Liz was the ticket taker. Tim and Larry, the copywriters, wrote the copy for all the movies in the Bijou catalog. Jeremy worked in customer service.

Some of the Carol's staff. The bar cat, Trash, is on David Boyer's lap, *photo courtesy of Allen* *Patrykus.*

"One Monday morning, Teddy came into my office and said, 'I don't think Jeremy will be in today. I don't know when he'll be back. We were at Carol's on Friday night, and he met a guy from Milwaukee, and he went there for the weekend. I tried this morning, but he isn't answering his phone, and he isn't home.'

"This went on for a week. We put up missing persons fliers. No word. So, I called the editor of the gay paper in Milwaukee and told him what was going on, and he said something like, 'This is so strange. This is probably the fourth or fifth call we've had here about young gay men disappearing.' So we sent fliers to post at the bars and bathhouses there in case anyone had seen him. About three weeks later, the whole Dahmer thing came out. Jeremy was the sweetest guy—quiet, shy, and very funny. It was so terribly sad. Awful. The entire office was devastated. Like I said, we were a family."

"When all this business started coming to light, the police began to listen," said Allen Patrykus. "One morning, Tim knocked on the door. We went to the police station and worked on a composite. Prior to being named, Dahmer was described as a male Caucasian, lean six feet in height, and wearing a gold T-shirt, green plaid shorts, and loafers at the time."

On July 26, the *Chicago Tribune* reported. "... Friends of Weinberger said they have spent the days since his disappearance circulating fliers with his picture and a description. Meanwhile, a police artist prepared a composite sketch of a man seen leaving Carol's with Weinberger the night he disappeared.

"There were few leads in the disappearance until Monday when friends of Weinberger were approached by Chicago police who had a photo of the man now being held in connection with the Milwaukee killings, sources said.

"Those friends, the last to see Weinberger before his disappearance, said the photo resembled Weinberger's companion who had told them he was from Milwaukee, sources said. ..." (Joan Latz Griffin and David Silverman, 'Missing Chicago man may be among victims.' *Chicago Tribune*, July 24, 1991).

Two days later, Dahmer confessed to the killing.

"All the Dahmer stuff went down in July, and we closed in October," said Patrykus. "It was not only the horrible loss that closed the bar, but it was also the news crews that hung around outside and tried to interview patrons going in and coming out. This was a gay bar; not that many people wanted to be on the news. The CBS News van was parked across the street most Friday and Saturday nights. It wasn't long before there

The author (right) with the late historian Rich Wilson (left) in front of the Carol's Speakeasy display at Gerber/Hart Library and Archives, from the author's collection.

was no money coming in. The closing party for Carol's was huge. You couldn't move. People were giving huge tips. The whole last week we were open, people brought in pictures they had taken over the years. Ralph Paul from *Gay Chicago* brought me an envelope of pictures taken at the bar. It was very emotional for me. I didn't want to leave. Richard and I had been there since the place opened. I thought about all the good times we had there, all the rebuilding of the place, and all the decorations we had done. Now, it was all over, and it ended in this awful way, and at the same time, people were dying.

"Six months later, we still had our mailing list, so David Boyer set up a final farewell and customer appreciation party at an open space on Broadway. Many of us came together to work that one last night. That felt like something that needed to be done because the ending of Carol's was so abrupt."

After Carol's closed, that long piece of prime North Wells Street real estate remained vacant for 25 years. The building was not demolished. The brown wooden framed façade with the brick accent above the door remained, but it was never occupied or used again. In time, the paper covering the vertical window on the door fell away, offering a glimpse of the cavernous interior. Dust covered. Empty. It looked as though no one had crossed Carol's threshold since the day the club had closed. All things of value had long since been removed. In the filth on the floor were some dust-covered pages, a few wooden planks, and a couple of bricks—the debris of a bygone age. In 2016, after 25 years of sitting vacant, "the place where Chicago partied" was demolished.

...1980 as you walked towards the disco, you would hear the base of the music getting louder as you walked closer and closer. Finally, you could hear the song being played as you swung open the old wooden door, turning to your right and walking 6 or 7 steps, you had to present your membership card, and the door man would let you in. Overlooking the dance area you were greeted by multi-colored hues of flashing lights, music, people dancing, the fogginess of second hand smoke encasing the surroundings and of course all the smiles.... and as the giant disco ball slowly rotated, again casting a twinkle in your eye and thinking to yourself - "tonight's going to be another magical night. "- durkART

....and the music played as I danced for hours - the smiles, the laughter. I met new friends and reconnected with old acquaintances. I related to the lyrics of music and danced - the libations, new concoctions, my favorites and the shots I consumed, and I danced. If only time held still; of all the friends I knew, all the great times I shared, just a snap shot taken of romancing that era - now just a empty shell in my conscious - longing for those days of the music and dancing ...and life.

durkART® 2015
(abandoned 'for sale' building that housed Carol's Speakeasy in Chicago a very popular disco in the the eighties)

The Carol's facade with a parting memory, courtesy of durkART.

In a 2015 art piece, durkART wrote over an image of the vacant Carol's facade. "...And the music played as I danced for hours—the smiles, the laughter. I met new friends and reconnected with old acquaintances. I related to the lyrics of music and danced—the libations, new concoctions, my favorites, and the shots I consumed, and I danced. If only time held still; all the friends I knew, all the great times I shared, just a snapshot taken of romancing that era—now just an empty shell in my conscious—longing for those days of the music and the dancing...and life."

The Carol's Speakeasy staff, photo courtesy of Allen Patrykus

Bijou Theater

The Bijou Theater was two doors south of Carol's, on the ground floor of a four-story Victorian building at 1349 N. Wells. Ad copy for the

Sidewalk view along Wells St. of the Bijou Theater, courtesy of the Bijou.

newly opened Bijou read. "Extra, extra read all about it, better yet come and see what it is all about at Chicago's newest and most comfortable little theatre." The Bijou, which is French for "jewel," was originally slated to show underground films, but shortly after opening the theater began showing gay porn.

In 1971, Gene Siskel (1946-1999) wrote in his *Chicago Tribune* movies column. "A fire last March in Old Town's Piper's Alley destroyed the beginnings of a new kind of movie theater in Chicago. The proprietors of the Aardvark Theater were building a small theater to exhibit art films for which it had been difficult to secure local bookings. It was an exciting development.

"The site is covered with rubble, but the idea of a small art theater has risen from the ashes and opens tonight right down the block.

"Sean O'Conner, a former assistant manager of the Aardvark, has built the Bijou Theater, a 77-seat house (more like a large screening room) at 1349 N. Wells St., which he says is, 'dedicated to presenting unusual underground and foreign films...'" (Siskel, 'Bijou Bill of Fare.' *Chicago Tribune*, July 14, 1971).

In the August 1971 issue of the underground newspaper, the *Chicago Seed*, Janet described some of the Bijou interior. "The theater itself is newly remodeled. The walls are streaked with bright vibrant colors and the ceiling done in dark, heavy texture. One could be in a cave where water has exposed colored limestone in layers. The cave is covered with a plush yellow carpet. The Bijou is small, intimate, with seats for only 75. ..." When the piece in the *Chicago Seed* went to print there was an addendum. "(NOTE: As we went to press, the next feature at the Bijou was announced—it's turning into a porn house—don't go there.)" (Janet, 'The Bijou Theater.' *Chicago Seed*, Aug. 1971).

A short time after, Gene Siskel reviewed a triple feature playing at the Bijou. First on the bill was the underground film, *Tricia's Wedding*—a half hour parody by the queer San Francisco performance group, the Cockettes, on the White House marriage of Tricia Nixon Cox. *Tricia's Wedding* was followed by the 53-minute documentary, *S-M*. Third on the bill was Jean Genet's *Un Chant d'Amour* (1950). Of the three films, *S-M* was Siskel's favorite. (Siskel, 'The Movies.' *Chicago Tribune*, Sept. 6, 1971).

In 2011, Bijou owner Steve Toushin explained the origins of the Bijou. "I was involved in a theater called the Aardvark Theater in Piper's Alley. Underground films, which showed nudity, did exceptionally well.

My first arrest was on a film called *Flaming Creatures* (1963), which was a gay-themed film by Jack Smith.

"Things started changing in this world, and one of them was the opening of adult theaters, which then brought gay sexuality to the general public. I just couldn't walk in and get a theater license, so the first thing we put on was *Richard Nixon's Checkers Speech*. We put that on for about four or five weeks, then went right into adult films, always with gay content." (Forman, 'Bijou marks 40 years of controversy.' *Windy City Times*, July 27, 2011).

Steve Lutz first went to the Bijou in 1972. "I came to Chicago by train from Kansas City with my best friend. We looked at the movie section of the paper and saw the Bijou ad that said, 'All Male Cast.' I asked what that meant, and my friend said, 'What does it sound like?' So, of course, we went. I remember the heavy breathing in the audience. I remember because I had heard that was something that happened at adult films. We didn't do anything except look around and watch the movie. That was before they opened the upstairs."

"The Bijou customer, since the first day I opened the theater, has never been the young 18-to-25-year-old crowd," said Toushin. "The Bijou is too intimidating; young men have to get to know themselves better. We're always getting new people from Chicago who have heard of us or seen our ads. People are still coming out to the Bijou; we have a lot of return customers, regulars, married men, tourists who come to the big city to experience what they could never do back home, people who want to see porn in a sexual environment with other men, people that want anonymous sex." (Forman, 'Bijou marks 40 years of controversy, entertainment.' *Windy City Times*, July 27, 2011).

In 1973, the Bijou hosted the Midwest premiere of *Nights in Black Leather*, the first hardcore feature from Peter Berlin. "Peter Berlin came to Chicago one time to do some interviews at the theater. I was playing one of his films, and he walked into the back of the theater and then walked down and stood in front of the screen; everybody stood up and started applauding. He was dressed the exact same way he was on screen, so people thought he walked right out of the screen and into the Bijou. He was a gracious and a super man." (de la Croix, 'Chicago Whispers #192,' *Windy City Times*).

Born Armin Hagen Freiherr von Hoyningen-Henue in West Berlin, Germany in 1942. Armin eventually became "Peter Berlin," concocting the name because he was tired of having to repeat his real one. However, Berlin created more than just his name. He created a look and a persona. Berlin became master of his own image—a lean muscled object of desire, dressed for sex in leather or denim. Berlin became a symbol of heavy gay cruising and the overt gay sexuality of the 1970s. Berlin photographed himself, accentuating every muscle and bulge. As a "selfie" pioneer, Berlin branded his look with an end game of getting laid and in the process, he became a legend. His image was emblazoned upon the libidos of a gay generation. His image was as iconic as the drawings of Tom of Finland or the work of Chicago's own Etienne aka Dom Orejudos (1933-1991). Peter Berlin was iconic in the gay adult world despite the fact that he made only two XXX films in his heyday, *Nights in Black Leather* (1973), and *That Boy* (1974). He came to the Bijou for both of his feature films.

Toushin also enjoyed his dealings with the wonderful, crazy filmmakers back in the day. "Those men were very proud of the films they made. In those years, gay films in theaters were an event. Widely popular with internationally known stars, most of the films had storylines. Those early years produced strong, positive gay images— sexual images that were presented on the movie screens..." (Forman, 'Bijou Marks 40 years of controversy.' *Windy City Times*, July 27, 2011).

In 1972, and again in 1973, the Bijou also showed the groundbreaking gay erotic film *Boys in the Sand* directed by Wakefield Poole (1936-2021). Before Wakefield Poole, gay XXX was porn loops and poorly shot fuck films. In 1971, the former dancer and choreographer changed "the face" of gay porn. His film, *Boys in the Sand* was a well-lit, full-length, professionally scored gay porn movie—gay porn meant for the big screen. The film was a sensation, receiving mainstream press and celebrity attention. Liza, Halston, Nureyev, and John Gielgud attended screenings. With the release of the film, both Poole and the film's star, Casey Donovan (1943-1987), became sensations.

In 2019, Wakefield Poole shared a bit about the film. "My inspiration for *Boys in the Sand* was a film called *Highway Hustler*. I saw it with three friends... It was really bad, not erotic, and had no production values at all. We were bored, and after paying $5 each, we felt ripped off. I owned a 16mm camera... It started as an experiment, just to see if I could make a porno that wasn't sleazy and degrading. I have to say that my inspiration while making the film was Cal Culver (aka Casey Donovan) and Fire Island itself. Together, they made magic.

"When my partner and I decided to go on with the project, I told him that we had to do it like a real movie. We both entered into it with no guilt about being gay or doing porn. We weren't doing a gay movie—we were making a movie for gays. We were doing something experimental and new. After the film opened, the word of mouth was unbelievable. Jerry Robbins' agent told me that after Jerry saw the film, he called Leonard Bernstein and said, 'Lenny, you have to go see it. It's wonderful. Beautiful men, good music, good sex, and it even has a plot!'

"When I made *Boys in the Sand*, I wanted to do a film with good-looking men that was well lit, had good production values, and something to engage the brain as well...Nowadays, there is beautiful work out there, but it has become formulaic and lacks warmth...I'm from the era when porn directors became independent filmmakers. Directors like J. Brian (1942-1985), Jack Deveau (1935-1982), Joe Gage, and Toby Ross all made gay cinema what it is today. I'm talking gay cinema, not porn." (Keehnen interview. *Grab Magazine,* 2019).

Chicagoan Don Bell went to school in Urbana. "In college, I discovered *After Dark* magazine. That was how I found out about gay life. Once, I took the train to Chicago to secretly see *Boys in the Sand* at the Bijou Theater. It starred Casey Donovan, and it was the first gay movie I ever saw that was not all grainy and in black and white. I remember when I entered the theater, the floor was sticky, and the seats were almost kind of crunchy sitting down. Men ended up sitting down beside me. I kept thinking, 'Okay, I have got to be cool. I am by myself. I cannot call for help.' I was sitting there, nervous and scared, and trying to tell myself to grow up. Finally, the movie started, and it was huge and golden and wonderful. I saw sex acts on screen I had not yet experienced or even imagined. The Bijou was a place of touching. There was no talk there, no one sought consent—they just had one another. Then I went to the bathroom, and it was another outrageous visual feast. I was hesitant, but mostly because I was inexperienced. I was on sensory overload. I was a cinema devotee, so when the movie ended, I waited to see every bit of the closing credits, and then I got up and left. I had to catch the train back to Urbana."

When *Boys in the Sand* returned to the Bijou Theater in 1973, the showing was a double feature. Second on the bill was Poole's XXX follow-up feature, the appropriately titled, *Bijou*. Despite the name, *Bijou* had nothing to do with the theater.

In addition to Berlin, early gay adult film legends to appear at the Bijou included Al Parker (1952-1992), Jim Cassidy aka Rick Cassidy (1943-2013), Richard Locke (1941-1996), and performer/director Fred Halsted (1946-2009). The theater was soon being described in newspaper ads as, "The theater that brought you—*Boys in the Sand, Adam and Yves, Cruisin' 57, Ballet Down the Highway*, and *Left Handed*." In other words, the Bijou Theater was a prime venue for the booming genre. Other popular features at the theater included *Centurions of Rome, A Night at the Adonis*, and the iconic Joe Gage XXX trilogy of *Kansas City Trucking, El Paso Wrecking Company*, and *L.A. Tool and Die*.

Bijou advertisement, showing the 1349 N. Wells St. building, , courtesy of the Bijou.

Bruce Vilanch lived in Old Town from 1970 to 1975. "I lived at 61 E. Goethe, then 1616 N. Wells, then 1636 N. Wells. I used to wander down to the Bijou. There was a cat lady with a store down there (the Feline Inn, 1445 N. Wells), and I would stroll down there as an excuse— then go to the Bijou. I liked it because the guys were in the theater and in the restroom. There was an overhead light in that hallway that led back to the restroom. Almost every time I was there, some guy would be posing in that archway. The men there were more than willing to go back to the bathroom with you. I bought magazines there too—*Drummer* and others, the full scope. Different places could mail magazines in a plain brown wrapper, but a lot of guys came in to buy them because they couldn't risk having them mailed."

In July 1972, Robert Davis reported for the *Chicago Tribune* that, "A federal grand jury will open an investigation next week into the showing of hardcore pornographic films in Chicago area theaters, United States Atty. James R. Thompson announced yesterday."

Thompson (1936-2020), who five years later became the Governor of Illinois, claimed that at least a dozen Chicago theaters were showing such films. Thompson took city authorities to task for not, "trying to curb the 'burgeoning growth of hard-core pornography in the Chicago area...'"

Hours prior to Thompson's decree, the owners of two Chicago adult movie theaters were ordered to appear in Federal District Court, "to show cause why films currently showing at their theaters should not be confiscated." (Davis, 'U.S. to Probe Showing of 'Adult' Movies Here.' *Chicago Tribune*, July 25, 1972).

A month later, Davis reported that a federal judge ordered the seizure of four adult films from two theaters because 'they were probably obscene.' "In addition to the Bijou, the other theater named in the warrant and seizure was the Admiral Theater (3940 W. Lawrence). The Bijou voluntarily turned over *Ranch Slaves* and three short films. However, the Admiral refused to turn over its three films in question— *Deep Throat*, *Kiss This Miss*, and *Vacation in Hotpants*." Davis goes on to say that the seizure of the films was only the first step in the announced crackdown on films showing hardcore porn in Chicago by the U.S.

attorney's office. (Davis, 'Judge OKs Smut Film Seizures.' *Chicago Tribune*, Aug. 1972).

Months later, Richard Cross wrote in the *Chicago Tribune Magazine*, "The all-out 'smut war' envisioned when the Supreme Court tightened obscenity rules never did take place in the weeks that followed—no spectacular raids, no dramatic courtroom scenes, no attention-getting 'sweeps' or 'crackdowns.' There were, however, a number of quiet, methodical arrests, and a lot of people in Toushin's business found themselves facing so many indictments that they could hardly keep track of them all.... (Cross, 'Busting the blue movie.' *Chicago Tribune Magazine*, Dec. 2, 1973).

The year 1974 brought trouble of a different sort. *The Daily Herald* reported, "Two adult theaters were bombed and a fire was found at a third, all minutes apart Thursday night. Another bomb was found less than an hour later at a fourth adult theater. One person was injured. The first explosion rocked the Rialto Theater (546 S. State) in the Loop, but no one was injured. A small fire was found a few minutes later on the roof of the Follies Theater (450 S. State). No damage was done. Another explosion occurred at the Newberry Theater (854 N. Clark St.) on the Near North Side, injuring one person. A bomb was planted at the Bijou Theater, but only blasting caps went off." ('Loop theaters hit by bomb, arson.' *The Daily Herald*, Nov 15, 1974).

The *Tribune* reported that the blasts all occurred within 10 minutes of one another. "Less than 10 minutes after the Newberry explosion, Keith Allison, manager of the Bijou Theater, 1349 N. Wells St., heard a small pop and smelled an odor like exploded fire crackers, police said." Three sticks of dynamite and a one-pound charge of TNT were found. (Mitchell Locin and Howard Marks, 'Bombs rock 3 porno houses; dynamite sticks found in 4th.' *Chicago Tribune*, Nov 15, 1974).

There were whispers of the mob or a madman. At the time, the possibility was also floated about that the bombs were the result of recent problems with the projectionists' union. Despite the troubles, business at the Bijou was on the rise. A big city like Chicago offered anonymity.

In the 1970s, gay travel became popular. Gay people wanted to experience gay life in other cities. Annual gay travel guides emerged like the *Bob Damron Address Book,* which started secretly in 1965. *The*

Spartacus Guide began in 1970 and offered listings of gay spots worldwide. *The Gay Yellow Pages* began publication in 1974. Gay bars and bathhouses often topped the list of things to do on "gaycations." When visiting Chicago, the gay spots of note included the Bijou.

In 1973, the Bijou Theater was mentioned in one of the first issues of the gay travel magazine, *Ciao!* Reviewer for the magazine, Ralph W. Davis, wrote, "Strictly gay films here. A nice crowd of gays and some very heavy cruising and action in the theater. The peep show next door is popular for the quick, stand-up jobs in the booth."

Another reason for the uptick in business was that the Bijou advertised. Ads for the theater often included eye-catching graphics from the featured film. David F learned of the Bijou from the newspapers. "I remember a movie ad with a photo of Jack Wrangler (1946-2009)— seductive, masculine. I had minimal experience, but I made up for it in desire. The price to get in was nothing, $5 maybe."

Ron V was aware of the Bijou from the ads in the *Chicago Sun-Times*. "My friend and I went to the Bijou when I was home on college break. The movie was *Men of the Midway* (1983). We were very naïve. We sat and watched the movie and left. I got the *Chicago Sun-Times* at college and I started to clip and save the Bijou ads. I did that for probably four years. I liked the look of the ads.

Jimmy D'Ambrosia remembered that even advertising the name of the current feature could sometimes be controversial. "There was an issue about the *Chicago Sun-Times* refusing to advertise *Rear Admiral* (1990), but Steven Toushin refused to censor the titles of his films."

The Bijou phone line was another form of advertising. Hearing about the current features at the Bijou Theater was as simple as dialing 943-5397.

"In sixth grade, the phone ads for the Bijou were all the rage," said Steve Migalski. "Kids at school would call the number and listen and giggle. I called it at home. That phone message was a glimpse of something amazingly queer in my world. I didn't know anything else. I called that number weekly for six years, until I was out of high school. For years that was my only connection to anything queer."

"I was the voice of the Bijou for a while," said Mike Donner. "Every week, Steve Dahl from the WLUP, the Loop, would call and play our outgoing message listing the current features. Then he would make fun of it on the air. I was working at the Bijou, and I had a theater background, so I asked Steven (Toushin) if I could write a script for the outgoing message and do character voices. He let me do it. A couple of my characters were Southern Stanley and Skippy Goodie Mood. I would record the messages and do silly scenarios and things. Steve Dahl still called the Bijou box office every week, but now at least we were in on the joke. That part of his broadcast became quite popular. At the time, I was still closeted. One day, my brother and sister-in-law called me. When I answered the phone, they said, 'Is this Jock LaRock Cocoa from the Big Boy Bulging Biceps Gym?' They had heard the Bijou message on the radio."

Jiminez De Oaxaca learned about the Bijou from the Steve Dahl broadcast. "Every week, he would call and listen to the Bijou-recorded message of the current attractions. I called the theater to find out the address. Once I got inside, I was determined to see every inch of the place.

The façade of the Bijou was nothing remotely flashy. The entrance was a simple step-up doorway. The Bijou sign was supported above the entrance to the theater by chains. The suspended sign was turquoise blue with "Bijou" scrawled in cursive pink neon—which was less garish than it sounds. A modest letter board in the display window displayed the current features and show times.

The Theater Bijou sign, courtesy of the Bijou.

"I always liked the window displays," said Tim G. "The tasteful storefront façade with that little flower arrangement and the board with the black and white letters of the current feature."

"I loved the cute neon sign," said David Plomin. "I liked the window display as well and the tasteful vase and flowers with only the name of the movie. I always figured they were trying to go under the radar. The people who needed to know knew about it."

The Bijou Theater front display window, courtesy of the Bijou.

Mike Donner recalled watching men approach the theater from the nearby Bijou offices and Video Sales a couple doors north at 1363 N. Wells. "We always used to crack up because the guys would always look both ways over their shoulder before pressing the button to be buzzed inside."

In the early 1990s, Jimmy Doyle had a friend who lived above the Bijou. "When she would go to smoke on the fire escape in the front, she would see guys entering the Bijou with their heads down. She wanted them to hold their heads high. 'Walk proudly, boys' was what she said she wanted to shout to them. She was my first sex-positive friend."

Welcome to the Bijou.

Press Bell to Enter.

David Plomin described the setup. "As you entered, the ticket booth was on the right. There was a ticket taker at the front and a booth with a glass front, and you passed your money through the opening at the bottom."

"The Bijou ticket booth was like something out of the 1950s," recalled Markt. "It had a half-moon opening for the money, the whole deal. The Bijou had a small lobby and a curtain in the doorway to the theater to block the light. Other than that, I don't remember much about the downstairs. I always headed straight upstairs."

In the early years, the lobby contained pulp novels, sex toys, and magazines. Eventually, much of the space for pulp novels and other print materials made way for the VHS phenomenon. When that occurred, the walls themselves became a 3-D Bijou sales and rental catalog.

As David Weeks described, "The lobby was wallpapered with images from the Bijou Video Sales Catalogue, and each image had the film catalog number on it."

"The movie box covers and posters were everywhere," added Ron V. "There was a visual catalog as well to flip through to see what you wanted to rent."

"There were DVD cases and racks and racks of cardboard DVD boxes in the lobby, too," said David F. "The gay papers were there—Gay Life and Gay Chicago. Maybe a couple titles like Midwest Swingers."

"I was so green about porn videos," recalled Paul Richardson. "I bought a VHS tape there, took it home, watched it, and brought it back. I tried to return it. They just stared at me and said, 'Video purchases are final.' I was horrified. I couldn't keep it. I was still living at home. Eventually, I threw out my entire porn collection by zipping it inside a beanbag chair and throwing that away."

"The Bijou was some money to get in, but once you were inside it was all free," said Malone Sizelove. "There was always a sparse older crowd downstairs in the theater. At first, I wasn't sure how it worked there. Do you go and sit down next to someone? Do you lean against the walls like in Brazil?"

The first all-male adult theater Danny K visited in Chicago was the Newberry (856 N. Clark Street). "I was so nervous. I had never seen porn on a big screen before. This was pre-Internet, so it's hard to imagine the impact of gay porn on the big screen. I liked the Newberry, but I never went back. By then, I had discovered the Bijou."

The Newberry Theater featured "all the best in all male films."

The Newberry opened in 1914 with seating for 700. By the early 1970s, it had become a gay adult movie theater with new features every Friday. (Cinema Treasures.org).

Given the theater's proximity to the Hancock Building, the Newberry advertised in the gay press as, "The Newberry Theater, located at the base of the 'cock'."

In 1975, *Chicago Tribune* film critic Gene Siskel covered the Newberry as well as the Bijou in one of his movie columns. "There are two movie theaters in Chicago that show feature-length gay films: the Newberry, 865 N. Clark St., and the Bijou, 1349 N. Wells St…. This does not include the dozens of sex book stores with peep show booths offering 90 seconds of gay and straight sex films for 25 cents.

"The Newberry, immediately west of Bughouse Square, is the bigger and less attractive of Chicago's two gay theaters.

"Like the Bijou, the Newberry charges $4 for admission to a two-hour program that includes one feature and one or two shorts. Unlike most heterosexual porno houses, neither the Newberry nor the Bijou has a candy or popcorn counter. And yet, according to industry sources, the gay film houses generally do slightly better business than their straight counterparts. The reason: Gays use the Newberry and Bijou as meeting places. The Bijou… has a free coffee lounge in a room behind its screen; the Newberry has placed four chairs in an alcove in the corner of its lobby.

"Inside the theaters the differences between gay and straight porno audiences are not immediately noticeable. With both kinds of movies, the audience is overwhelmingly male. The age and racial mixture is as wide as you can imagine. 'We've got one old guy who walks in here with two canes,' said a Newberry ticket-taker.

"The majority of customers sit alone and away from each other. A deadly quiet hangs in the air. In line with their function as a meeting place, however, there is some verbal contact between patrons of gay theaters. A few customers constantly cruise the aisles soliciting companionship. Says a manager of the Bijou: 'The biggest difference is the audience for straight and gay films is that the straights want to be alone with their sexual fantasies on the screen, whereas some of the gays want to act out their fantasies at home with members of the audience'..." (Siskel, 'The gay porno market: Shoddy, self-sustaining.' *Chicago Tribune*, Aug. 24, 1975).

Beyond the Newberry ticket counter was a metal turnstile for admittance with a sign that said, "No ins and outs!" Admission was $4. A plainclothes cop was often seated on a stool at the entrance. The theater was open noon until midnight. In 1973, *Ciao*, gave the Newberry Theater a quick but telling review, "Hustlers can get rough in the john! The theater can be wild!" The Newberry closed in 1976/1977. Shortly after, a sign went up, "Watch for the Grand Reopening." It never came. Months later, the Newberry was demolished.

As mentioned, the Newberry Theater was across from another sexually active area for gay men, Bughouse Square. Also known as Washington Park (901 N. Clark Street), Bughouse Square was a center of gay cruising and hustling for decades.

In his groundbreaking 1963 novel, *City of Night*, award-winning gay author John Rechy described the hustler scene at Bughouse Square. "Hunting eyes outline the ledges of the park. Male hustlers assume that tough veneer of hoods. After two in the morning, cars still go around the block to choose a paid partner from the stagline. New in town...I splashed on the scene, going from morning to morning—in and out of different cars that stopped after circling the block." (Rechy, *City of Night*. Grove Press, 1963)

In *States of Desire*, literary legend and former Chicagoan Edmund White wrote, "One of my frequent hangouts was Bughouse Square, a city block frequented by soap box orators and hustlers. I hired quite a few of those boys, many of whom were several years older than I. In those days they all pretended to be straight, spat frequently and permitted themselves to be done, nothing more. When I revisited the square, at the corner of Delaware and Dearborn, I found about forty hustlers cruising at eight on a Sunday evening. All of them were parading along the periphery of the park, not in it; they wanted to be visible to johns passing by in their automobiles..." (White, *States of Desire*. E.P. Dutton, 1980).

On June 27 1970, Bughouse Square was also the starting point for Chicago's first Pride March. The event was called a march and not a parade because people remained on the sidewalk instead of walking in the street. As the step-off site for the March, Bughouse Square became an area for the pre-march rally with speeches by a roster of community leaders and activists.

"Bughouse Square, long infamous as a Chicago cruising and hustling park for gays, was a natural location for the rally, marking the first anniversary of homosexuals renouncing the guilt, repression, fear and shame that that park represents..." (Richard Larsen, 'Chicago Gay Liberation.' Chicago Seed, June 1970).

With the advent of gay liberation, there were suddenly dozens of less risky options for gay men seeking sex or looking to engage hustlers. There were bars and bookstores and classified ads in the gay papers. Chicago also had a large number of gay bathhouses like Man's Country (5015-17 N. Clark St.), the Wacker Baths (674 ½ N. Clark St.), Club Baths Chicago (609 N. LaSalle), and C.H.A.P.S. (116 W. Hubbard). And in Chicago, there was also the Bijou—a theater and sex club where, unlike the Newberry, business was thriving.

In 1976, the Bijou was back in the news. *The Daily News* reported that part owner Paul Gonski was shot in a lot near the theater. "The head of a string of hard-core pornographic movie theaters was shot and killed Tuesday in what appeared to be a Chicago gangland fashion. Police in a passing patrol car discovered Paul M. Gonsky, 34, lying beside his expensive foreign car in a parking lot in the nightclub area of Old Town. Gonski had been shot seven times—six times in the head and once in the shoulder. He died about three hours later in Henrotin Hospital."

The Daily Herald reported, "The Bijou is one of a number of theaters specializing in X-rated movies which are owned by Festival Theaters Corp. Police suspected Gonsky might have been killed because he resisted attempts by the Chicago crime syndicate to let 'the outfit' in on a slice of the pornography profits.' (Metropolitan briefs, 'Head of X-rated movie houses killed.' *The Daily Herald*, Sept. 22, 1976).

The next day, *The Daily Herald* printed the following, "Paul Gonsky, the kingpin of Chicago's pornographic movie theaters, apparently knew his killer and knew he was a 'hit' target before he was shot down with seven bullets in the Old Town night club district, police said Wednesday. Gonsky, 34, who started as a promoter of 'art' movies and would end up running the city's biggest string of 'skin houses,' was killed Tuesday as he locked the door of his expensive foreign car close by the Bijou, a theater specializing in homosexual films which he controlled.

"Homicide Commander Joseph Di Leonardi said: 'We believe he knew his killer. We believe he knew he was a target. The man was carrying a pistol, so he surely knew his life was in danger. It's all an assumption, but apparently he knew the man who shot him." ('Porno film king knew his killer.' *The Daily Herald*, Sept. 23, 1976).

A couple of days later, the *Chicago Tribune* followed up, "Porno theater operator Paul Gonsky met with a middle-echelon crime syndicate hoodlum who demanded money from him several days before he was gunned down in an Old Town parking lot, police disclosed Friday.

"Investigators said the hoodlum ordered Gonsky to pay $300 a week in what they termed, 'an obvious shakedown attempt by the Young Turks of the mob.'

"The meeting took place Sept. 17 in Gonsky's office above the Bijou Theater, 1349 N. Wells, a witness told police.

"Gonsky, 34, was found shot to death Tuesday in a parking lot at 1317 N. Wells St." (Philip Wattley, 'Police say hoodlum asked sex theater exec for money.' *Chicago Tribune*, Sept. 25, 1976).

Richard F didn't go to the Bijou frequently. "The Bijou wasn't convenient, but I liked the different atmospheres it provided. I had been to the Newberry Theater and was cruising there with the whole thing of moving closer and then knees touching, the side glances, and the stray hand, all that. At the Newberry, they had someone who kept an eye on the bathroom. It all felt very risky there. Then someone told me about the Bijou.

"Going to the Bijou provided that adult theater experience, watching the cruising in the theater and vibing off the energy. Being there, it felt like sexual freedom and, on some level, that we were expressing our right to pleasure without shame. Upstairs at the Bijou was something else. Upstairs was just fun. I am not big on glory holes, but I was a big fan of cruising and feeding off that energy too. The place was like a quieter version of Man's Country. There was little talking going on there that I remember."

"At the Bijou," Toushin explained, "we had a little bit of cruising in the back and the bathrooms, then in '78, I put some booths in, and they went over well. It was around 1981 that I opened up the second floor." (de la Croix, 'Chicago Whispers #192,' *Windy City Times*).

Prior to the opening of the second-floor playroom, the Bijou Theater was not open 24 hours a day, seven days a week. Instead, the Bijou had hours reflective of the typical film showing times of 7 p.m., 8:45 p.m., and 10:30 p.m.

In 1983, award-winning independent gay porn director William Higgins (1942-2019) made a personal appearance at the Bijou to promote his newest film, *Class Reunion,* starring Michael Christopher, who was also scheduled to appear. Higgins was a force in the gay porn world with hits like—*Boys of Venice* (1978), *Pacific Coast Highway* (1981), and *A Sailor in the Wild* (1983). Christopher was a popular gay adult film entertainer of the period whose credits included *The Best Little Warehouse in L.A.* (1982), *Gayracula* (1983), and *Pleasure Beach* (1983).

Jimmy D'Ambrosia shared an anecdote about the event. "Steve Toushin was giving William Higgins a tour of the building, and Michael Christopher came a little later and buzzed the door. Jimmy R was at the ticket booth. Michael Christopher was trying to explain to Jimmy that he was here with William Higgins and that he was the star of the movie being shown. But Jimmy had heard nothing about that, so he just kept saying, 'I don't care who you are, nobody comes in or gets in for free unless Steve Toushin tells me so. I do my job.' Michael Christopher eventually just paid the $8 for admission. And then, when William Higgins and Steven came back, Jimmy would not let it go. He kept saying, 'Am I wrong? You pay me to take tickets and you said no one gets in for free. Was I wrong? Was I wrong to make him pay?"

Patrick Hughes liked to go upstairs at the Bijou but not to play. "I liked to go there as just a weird thing to do. It was a kind of tourism for me. There was not a right angle in the place, and it was so dark."

"I remember the smell of the place the first time I walked inside," recalled Victorino. "It was poppers, man, and ass—an interesting smell.

The kind of smell that made me think, this is going to be good. The floor was sticky and the walls in the theater were a deep maroon, or that was just the color they became after years of nicotine and poppers."

Daniel L recalled lots of fooling around in the movie. "But it was too strange for me to do anything. After I started school in the city, I went there more often. I was a romantic. I went there looking for love because I didn't know any better. The Bijou was my introduction to a lot of things. I thought that was gay life. Men were against the walls by the bathroom. I discovered the upstairs later. At the start, I went there looking for love. Once I started going to bars, I didn't go to the Bijou much anymore. Love seemed more likely to happen at a bar."

Advertisement for Michael, Angelo, and David (1976) showing at the Bijou, including a live appearance by Marc Stevens, courtesy of the Bijou. The Bijou frequently hosted appearances by various gay adult film stars as well as gay film directors.

"The theater was small, and the screen was fairly small too," recalled David Plambeck. "The cloth seats were spongy, and the sound of the movies was horrible. The first few times I went there I watched the movie and beat off. It was later that they added a maze upstairs for adult play."

"The first time I went to the Bijou, I saw *Blondes Do It Best* (1985), said Jimmy D'Ambrosia. I remember the Jeff Stryker movie *Powertool* (1986) being huge there and *Powertool 2* (1992). We also sold the Jeff Stryker dildo, which was $79 back then." When Stryker appeared at the Bijou to promote his films, he signed his dildos as well." The Jeff Stryker Cock and Balls molded dildo was huge in size (10.5" x 2") as well as in popularity. The Stryker dildo came with an autographed photo.

Joey McDonald was fresh from a stint in the Navy when he first went to the Bijou in 1976. "I went to see a porn movie about a drag queen." The film was Jack Deveau's 1974 feature, *Drive*, which is described by Movie Database as a film about a drag queen named Arachne who tries to take over the world by stealing a drug that zaps people's sex drive, but secret agent Clark is out to stop her.

"The theater was so dark that it took your eyes a while to adjust," recalled Dean Ogren. "The aisle was on the right, and it ran to the front of the theater and behind the screen. I went there a couple of times to see some classics like Joe Gage's *L.A. Tool and Die* and anything with Jack Wrangler."

When asked, on the 40th anniversary of the Bijou, what were the most popular films to play there, Toushin replied, "Most popular porn movies that have been shown at the Bijou: *Centurions of Rome* (1981), *Night at the Adonis* (1978), The Gage Brothers Trilogy—*El Paso Wrecking Company* (1978), *L.A. Tool and Die* (1979), *Kansas City Trucking (1976)*, *Wanted* (1980) and *The Idol* (1979)." (Forman, 'Bijou Marks 40 years of controversy.' *Windy City Times*, July 27, 2011).

David D would get horned up at Carol's and then head over to the Bijou. "After the first time, I learned to pick an aisle seat. You didn't want to be trapped, landlocked by some guy with aggressive hands. I didn't mind. I have a big dick, so it was nice to give them a little candy, maybe a feel. I was very much about safe sex at the time. I was visual anyway. I loved the erotic energy there. The Bijou was a place where I realized my sexual power in a way."

Bijou membership card, courtesy of the author's collection.

"Once, when they tried to bust the place, the cops came in and confiscated the film," said Carl R. "It was hilarious because the film playing was a gay porn movie, but it was this story about the challenges of coming out. In other words, it was a film with redeeming social value, so the case was thrown out.... The first time I stepped into the darkness of the theater, I was so nervous. There was a moment of blindness before my eyes adjusted. What was I walking into? What seats were empty? I could not believe I was seeing anal sex on screen. I took a seat, and then someone sat next to me, and I had to decide whether to move or stay. If I stayed, there would be leg contact; a hand would come over and then move higher. I was never the aggressor in that sort of thing."

John Barak first went to the Bijou in 1974. "I'd seen the ads for the movies in the paper, and the guys looked so hot that I decided to just do it. I went and had a seat, and a guy came over and sat down next to me. He reached over and felt me. Until then, no guy had ever even touched my dick before. I was already turned on by the movie, so when he went down on me, it didn't take long. It was sweet. He even had a little towel to wipe up. Then he said, 'My turn.' I said I needed to hit the bathroom and then booked it. I did that two or three times before I started meeting guys when I went out to the bars."

"In the theater, I got more action in the back," said David Plomin. "Guys would come in, see a shadow looking at them, and sit nearby. If they were interested, they would come over or give me the look. If I was interested, I would move over. Then, when we were close, it was legs touching and hand on thigh. If there's still not flinching, up to the crotch. Then we would head to the bathroom or an upstairs booth."

The downstairs bathroom at the Bijou was behind the screen with two urinals and one stall with an enormous glory hole. "I used to go to that bathroom and sit on the toilet and play with people before going upstairs," said Rail.

Steve Lutz recalled consistent action there. "The bathroom was so tiny, but most times, it was wild in there. The downstairs bathroom was where I saw watersports for the first time. There was a guy who sat on the toilet facing the urinal who wanted people to pee in his mouth."

"I walked in there one night wearing a tuxedo," said Greg McFall. "I had come straight from an event. I was about to go upstairs, but I went to the bathroom first. In the bathroom was a friend of mine who was also at the event that night and also in a tuxedo. He was lying on his back on the Bijou bathroom floor rimming some guy in leather."

The narrow hallway beyond the bathroom led to the outside area. When the Bijou patio opened in 1980, the back area was referred to in the media as the summer frolic garden. Soon it was better known as the sex garden. The back area was open year-round for patrons to smoke, get fresh air, chat, and carry on al fresco.

"I liked the back garden area," said Chuck P Kass. "There was sex going on, but the Bijou also got a lot of closeted guys, so it could be a lot of meet and greet and talking and hanging out by the pop machine. There was a whole population there who wanted to connect and be a little social—a lot of married men and out-of-towners who were a little lonely or wanted to know what to do in Chicago."

Ian Lobell recalled the sex garden. "It was such a contrast to the inside because the gardens were actually very tended with trimmed hedges and flowerbeds, so cruising and messing around back there felt strange—it wasn't what you would expect, at least I didn't."

"There were little coves in the hedges and blind spots back there," said Robert Kimmons. "I was very cautious. There were windows in the buildings around that could see what was happening." The sex garden was indeed nestled near several taller buildings, including a few high-rises to the east.

Ron V liked to escape to the Bijou patio for fresh air. "There was a weird hedge maze back there. At night, full-on sex would happen back there, but not during the day. The neighboring buildings could have seen. A sign on the back patio read, 'Please Be Respectful of Our Neighbors.' There was a 'Beware of Pickpockets' sign back there too." Ron V added that patrons of the Bijou could also access the second floor playroom from the patio, "If you didn't want to navigate the winding stairs. There was a wooden stairwell off the patio, the kind that is on the back of brownstones, so you could go up to the landing on the second floor and go in that way. The back stairs had a locked gate going to the third floor, so unless you had a key, you could only go to the Bijou playroom. If you were already up there, you could come out on the back landing and look down on the garden."

"Light streamed into the play area sometimes during the day when that door was open," recalled Ivan Lozano. "You could look down into the garden and watch the people smoking and cruising outside."

"Sometimes, when I was hard up for money," added Greg McFall. "I would wear something loose and climb over the wall in the alley to the Bijou back area. People would come to the back to smoke and cruise, sometimes a little more. After I snuck into the garden, I would just go into the theater through that back door."

Nels Highberg added, "During summer, they brought three or four booths with glory holes out to that patio area and put them along the brick walkway."

"For a while in the summer, Steve Toushin had hot dogs and hamburgers back there on Sunday afternoons," recalled Jimmy D'Ambrosia.

"In the back, I fucked a guy ass up on a bicycle," recalled Bill Silver. "Part of the excitement of fucking him was the guys standing outside smoking who were encouraging us."

Bob M went outside to smoke and to cruise. "Going outside was nice because you could see who you were hooking up with. Sometimes, I didn't like to know who it was, and I didn't want to know what they looked like."

A Bijou theater advertisement, courtesy of Gay Chicago.

"In the 1990s, the Bijou added strippers, mainly the men who were in the movies produced with Toby Ross, Michael Donner, etc. The stripper shows were presented four days a week, in the afternoons and evenings." (Forman, 'Bijou marks 40 years of controversy, entertainment.' *Windy City Times,* July 27, 2011).

Victorino was a theater major in college when he saw an advertisement for dancers in the back of the free gay Chicago paper, *Babble.* "When I went for the interview, I forgot my ID. Steve Toushin did not believe I was of age. I had the interview and then came back the next day for the final paperwork and to show them my license. When I handed my ID to the guy doing the paperwork, he shouted, 'He's legit' loud enough that Steve could hear him in his office next door.

"When I came in for my shift, I gave my cassette to the person at the ticket booth," continued Victorino. "I believe the person at the ticket counter also controlled the stage lights and the music. A few songs I did were '100% Pure Love' by Crystal Waters, 'Throb' by Janet Jackson, and Ce Ce Peniston's 'You've Got to Show Me Love.' We changed from street clothes into our stripper clothes in this little room back by the bathrooms that had lockers. Then you took the key. I remember because I danced with it around my ankle inside my cowboy boot.

"The house was dark when the movie was playing. When we danced there was a light over the proscenium stage. I liked the stripping because it helped flesh out the 20-minute set. I wore a short-sleeved button-down shirt that I unbuttoned and tossed aside, a tank top, Daisy Duke cutoffs, boots, and a jockstrap. Sometimes, I also wore a harness. I never went naked at the Bijou, but the gentlemen could feel the goods in a jockstrap—and nakedness depends on what you want to touch. The pay wasn't much, but the tips could be great. Lap dances were how you made bigger money. It might not sound like a lot today, but I remember walking out of there with $195 for 90 minutes of work.

"'Seasoned patrons would show their tip money first.' One of the guys I danced with at the Bijou told me to always see what they are tipping before they ask what you are willing to do. I never did anything extra for tips. It would have been easy, but I did not want to cross that line. Most dance shifts were 20 minutes for each dancer. The most strippers I ever worked with in a night there were two others. Mostly, we did a round robin. When one of us finished on stage, we would go work the crowd, and then the other would come on stage. There was a break, and then we would have another show later. Sometimes on weekends, the Bijou had porn star headliners—those nights, we were basically the opening act. I don't recall ever dancing with the porn stars."

Victorino took his job stripping as part of his theatrical training. "I even brought a good female friend, who I will call 'Q,' to the Bijou show. I wanted her to give me notes on my performance. Was my coy smile on point or too smarmy? I needed to discover the face that made me the most money. After we left the theater, I asked 'Q' about it, and she said, 'It's really not your face that they're looking at.'

"Something else about stripping there," he added, "was that the one aisle you took to get to the bathrooms and you took to get to the upstairs was also the aisle to and from our changing room. That meant it was the only way we had to leave the theater, which meant walking past the guys we had just stripped for. I tried to at least put on a ball cap when I was leaving. Usually, a couple of guys said hello as I went out, but mostly, I didn't want to break the illusion and the fantasy."

Steve Lutz recalled the shows. "They would dance on stage and then go into the audience, walking on the arms of the chairs to get to people. There was a lot of in-your-face action from the strippers there—but the strippers there tended to be twinks. My type of man was more the sort that went upstairs."

Tim G saw a show there with a friend from out of town. "We were a little drunk when we went. There were probably 20-25 men in the audience, most of them were near the front. We were further back in about the fifth row. The first guy came out with a dildo with a suction cup, stuck it to the stage, sat down, and fucked himself. Then he got up and started going through the audience. I was sort of shocked by that. The second stripper did a striptease and then went into the audience. The first guy he came to, sucked his dick, then the second guy, then third—then he went to the second row. He worked the crowd, seat by seat and row by row, and every guy was sucking his dick. I leaned over to my buddy and said, 'Girl, I know you like to suck dick—but no.'"

"The strippers couldn't be nude," recalled David F. "So a few just kept their socks on when they worked the crowd."

"I think we danced at 9 p.m., 11 p.m., and 1 a.m.," said Mercury. "I danced there a long time, so I had pretty much my pick of the shifts. We worked three dancers to a shift, 20 minutes each. Between sets, we sometimes went to the Chinese Restaurant that was right there beside the Over 21 and the Peeping Tom. "The owner was great; he would always say to us, 'Between sets?'" Mercury added that the Bijou often had a lot of tourists in the audience. "But there were a lot of regulars, too. Some of the guys were so nice. Sometimes, they even brought me a hamburger or something if I was dancing."

In the theater, sex rarely went further than a handjob or blowjob. At the Bijou, the real action was more likely to be happening on the second floor.

As Tay put it, "Upstairs at the Bijou was yum."

In 1980, Toushin expanded the Bijou, turning it into more of a sex club. "[The] Bijou did a good business once I opened up the second floor. I started picking up a lot of people from Carol's. When the bar closed, I had a huge surge of new customers. The party would finally quiet down around 9 or 10 a.m. in the morning. ..." (Forman, 'Bijou marks 40 years of controversy, *Windy City Times*, July 27, 2011).

"Coming out, I had such limited experience," said Robert Kimmons. "I had whatever was available, so random encounters in bathrooms, that kind of thing. I didn't know what to expect at the Bijou. I went there with a friend and we started watching the movie. I saw all these guys get up and go to the front and not come back. My friend asked if I wanted to see more. Then he took me upstairs. The smell was a blend of bleach, cigarette smoke, cum, sweat, and men. The whole idea of a place to go and just have sex was completely new to me. That day I had my first exposure to glory holes. I went in a booth and looked down, and a guy presented himself. I thought, 'What am I supposed to do?' As if on cure, he said, 'Suck it.'"

Danny K had been to the Bijou a few times before he discovered the bathrooms behind the screen and, subsequently, the spiral staircase leading to the second floor. "Of course, I went up. I was so nervous. I didn't know what I was walking into, but I climbed the stairs."

"On one end of the main room was a video screen with benches to watch the movie," recalled Kimmons, "Guys would stand along the wall. That room got very crowded. In the back of the second floor were a couple of slings and the maze and some booths that were chest height so you could kiss above the divider as well."

The first time I went to the Bijou," said Chris G, "I was sitting in the theater watching the movie and saw all these guys go behind the screen and not come back. I wondered where they all were going, so I wandered down behind the screen and discovered where everyone was going. I found the spiral staircase and then the glory holes. That was my first public blowjob. Once I found the second floor, I was out of my mind. I was intoxicated by the whole world of public sex. If music was playing, it wasn't playing very loud because I liked going up there sometimes and just listening to the sound of guys having sex."

"There was music upstairs," recalled Rail, "Not loud, but it was sex music, that thumping sleaze disco."

"The second floor brought out my darker and dirtier side," added Dean Ogren.

Beneath the spiral staircase was a soda machine. At the top of the stairs was a display case with a half wall behind it. The small sales kiosk was open weekends with a clerk on a stool behind the case. On display were lube, cock rings, toys, etc.

"They had real cans of Crisco in the display case," recalled Jimmy D'Ambrosia. "The small cans were $8, but they had larger cans too, those were $10-12. That little store had cock rings and poppers on ice. They also had hankies, a few dildos, and a couple of ball gags. Right next to the display case was a chair and a payphone that guys used to call when they were looking for hustlers. That payphone rang quite a bit. We always wondered how people got that number. The number of that phone was known to a lot of people."

Around the corner was the main room of booths with glory holes. The room had a high tin ceiling. Along one wall were two sets of bunk beds. The playroom featured a maze, a chain link fence, a St. Andrew's cross, a sawhorse, and a bathtub for water sports. The upstairs bathroom was primarily an inlet with a wall urinal.

The playroom was the stage for the unfolding of sexual fantasies, the exploring of kinks, and the satisfying of desires.

Tigg recalled booths. "Lot of booths. All sorts of booths—some with benches and some without. There were half booths, too. I remember a sling and the larger screen on the wall and a couple rows of viewing and blowing benches." The area with the large screen and viewing benches was known as the Circle J Theater.

"I liked standing at the door to a booth," said Jim P. "I would stand there and watch the movie at the end of the room, but I was cruising the crowd. When I saw a guy who was interested, I stepped back in the booth. Then the guy would come in and close the door."

Bob M remembers being on the bench and watching a movie. "This was in 1986 or so—a movie about gay Olympians with Al Parker (*Games*, 1983) was on the screen upstairs. AIDS terrified me. At the time, testing HIV positive was a death sentence, so I was extremely safe—which was frustrating. Anyway, I was jacking off on the bench watching this hot movie with Al Parker and was aware of the guys in the shadows watching. That was enough for me then, but it fulfilled being sleazy while being safe, which was a rare combination. When I was there, it was to watch and to show."

Steve Lutz recalled the graffiti in the upstairs booths. "You could see it once your eyes adjusted. Much of the graffiti was in ink and marker—quite a lot was carved into the wood fiber as well."

"I was upstairs on the bench watching the movie and this guy came over, took off my sneakers and socks, and went to town on my feet," recalled David Plomin. "It was so hot. I knew about foot stuff, but mostly I thought it was weird. I had no idea I could get off from it. To have a foot fetish and to get someone off who doesn't have a foot fetish, you have to be an artist. This man was an artist. I didn't explore the foot thing further, but after that, I understood how hot it could be."

Robert Kimmons shared an early experience at the Bijou. "A guy started kissing my neck, then my back, and then he started rimming me. I had no idea what he was doing—then I felt it and jumped. Was that his tongue on my butt? Later, I was blowing him, and when he got close, he grabbed the back of my head and held it in place. I had seen the movie *Cruising*, and I thought, 'Oh god, he is trying to kill me.' But he just wanted me to swallow."

Nels Highberg frequented the Bijou for a stretch in the 1990s. "I went after 11 p.m. because admission was cheaper. I would go upstairs and hang out mainly where the movie was playing. I was more into oral sex and the Bijou was ideal for that. Because of AIDS and HIV, when I was still in Houston, the slogan was 'cum on me not in me.' By the late 1990s, things started to change. I joked that at the Bijou I made up for all the swallowing I didn't do in Houston.

"The Bijou was good around 5 p.m. with guys stopping on their way home from work. Upstairs were full booths, some without doors and some chest-high so guys could stand there and get blown while they watched the movie. It was public and private sex at the same time. I tended to walk around. I fully bought into the dark and seedy feel. I loved how the sex there was just so honest about what it was. Making things

happen there was easy."

Advertisement featuring the 2nd floor Playspace and the Bijou Garden, courtesy of Gay Chicago.

Markt recounted, "I locked eyes with one guy—big mustache, jeans, cowboy boots, and this enormous belt buckle. He was just one of those wiry fuck boys. It was like magic. We began making out and this dominant part of me was unleashed. We drew quite a crowd. We were standing up. I was fucking him against that fence. We fucked for hours.

We would take a break and then go back at it. I've masturbated to that experience many times. It wasn't just the sex, it was all of it—it was the vortex of my confidence, self-esteem, and fantasies. That was the foundation of me starting to have gay sex without some form of shame."

David D had a trick when he saw two hot guys duck in a booth together. "I would wait a couple minutes and then knock. When they opened the door, I would show them my dick, and they would let me in. I told them I didn't want to participate but watch and masturbate. Most times they were cool with it. Most men liked having someone watching, encouraging them. I got into the talking-filthy part. They loved that and when they came, I would walk out the door."

"Upstairs at the Bijou came with quite a learning curve," offered David F. "Before going up there I wasn't even sure how to cruise. Curiosity caused me to catch on very quickly. Once, another guy and I started playing with each other, and soon it turned into a four or five-person orgy. It was thrilling to be a part of something so fun, safe, and naughty. I also got crabs at the Bijou a couple times."

Bill Silver added, "The Bijou is where I got my first case of gonorrhea. The first time I went there, I didn't realize there was anything more than the movie. So, I was sitting there watching the movie, and I kept seeing guys going down the aisle to the right of the screen. I figured out what was going on soon enough. I went upstairs and I remember thinking, 'all this for admission. I would have been fine seeing a couple of porn movies.' In the mid-1980s, I was quite a cocksucker and liked to fuck as well. The second floor was a real smorgasbord. It was like discovering paradise. I liked the sleazy feel. I met a number of people there. We were all just folks with different definitions of intimacy getting our needs met. I always felt good about going there. I dated one guy I met there. I thought I had met the love of my life, which might sound silly, but I really did have a sense that it was the kind of place where I might meet the love of my life. At first, it seemed incongruous to me that I might meet a nice guy there, but I was a nice guy, and I was there."

"The sling was on the right going back," recalled Jimmy D'Ambrosia. "The two sets of bunk beds were on the right, too. The mattresses on those were nasty."

"I would often come from work in a suit, so I would go in a booth and carefully fold my suit and sit and wait," said Greg McFall. "Or sometimes I wouldn't sit and wait. Sometimes I wouldn't even fold my clothes."

The Bijou was a popular spot for businessmen on their lunch hour. As David Plomin put it, "Nothing like a good-looking guy in a pair of tight polyester pants."

Rick Garcia had never been to a porn theater when he went to the Bijou with friends. "Shortly after we got there, my friends got up from watching the movie to walk around and did not come back. I decided I'd try to find where everyone was. I went upstairs. I heard a booth door open, and out came one guy and then another. Then, the door opened to the booth next door, and two guys came out of there, and then, finally, my friend Bob also came out there. He was a total mess, and the knees of his pants were filthy, and all he said was, 'I love it here.' All of us had very different reactions to going there. That friend adored it, another friend was disgusted, and my third friend said, 'Did you see that guy's feet in the movie?'"

In the early 1980s, Jamie Krohn sometimes went there after his bartending shift at the Gold Coast. "It was more social than anything. I went there after work with people. When you get off work at 5 a.m., there aren't a lot of places open. Most times we went to the Bijou we had done too much coke at the bar, and we weren't going to bed anytime soon."

"I don't drink or do drugs," said Jimmy Doyle. "The Bijou was my way of letting loose. Going up those winding stairs was like feeling the weight of the day fall away. Then it was this way if you want to have sex and see faces. And this way if you want sex, but only want to see cock. You could go and enjoy yourself at the Bijou, be there for 10 minutes, or be there for hours. There was a sense of community there with its own secret language. As someone raised Catholic, I felt it was almost sacramental. It felt like my truth, my rebellion, and hot sex combined. I liked being the exhibitionist and blowing some guy or getting blown in the theater."

Robert D. patronized the Bijou for the first time in the late 1980s. "I was at Carol's and decided to check it out. I went alone and was very nervous. I took a seat about six seats in. Ten minutes later, a naked man, wearing nothing but Converse All Stars, came crawling around the corner. He crawled over to me, unzipped my pants, and sucked me off.

Then he stood, and that was when I saw he was only wearing a cock ring. Then he ran to the front of the theater with his dick flopping around, went behind the screen, and disappeared. I thought, 'What the hell was that?' A few years later, I learned where he had vanished to and that there was more to the Bijou than I had thought. The maze, the booths—all of it was impressive. There were sturdily built bunk beds with shitty mattresses. This was no simple backroom."

"At first, I got off just watching because there was so much to see," said Jiminez De Oaxaca. "There were bunk beds. Slings. Booths. Lots of booths. There was a fence too, that involves a good sex story. In the bunk bed area, there was this football jock guy. I had been watching for a while and didn't feel like watching anymore. We started making out, and then I was fucking him while he was holding on to the chain link fence. People were watching. I liked that. I took him to where I was staying, and we fucked all night. The next morning, he called his buddy and told a story about meeting this girl and spending the night at her place.

"The Bijou became a funny thing with my friends. When they dropped me off at the end of the night, it was a standing joke that they drop me off at the Bijou. I liked having sex in those booths with men watching through the peepholes. That was really hot to me. I didn't usually do poppers, but one night I was doing them and fucking some guy in a booth, and the orgasm was so intense, I blurted out, 'I love you.' That was strange and surprising, but it just felt so good."

"Humping someone in a stall isn't always intimate," added Ian Lobell, "but when it is, it's transcendent and magical."

Bill Silver recalled the upstairs, "The maze was chest high, and I would see guys standing, waiting for whoever to come their way."

David D loved watching guys get blown up there, "I wanted to do more, but I was afraid of AIDS. I wanted to be a slut, but I absorbed a lot from that atmosphere. I got creativity from that environment."

"Each time I was in there, I was wasted," said Allen Patrykus. "One time I was in there, I saw Michael K in a sling on the second floor with a cast on his leg. And he said, 'I see you, Allen.'"

"The Bijou was as seedy as I expected," shared David Weeks. "But I was disappointed that it wasn't more of a happening place. I met a guy that first time. I saw him when I came out of the bathroom, and we played around for a while in a booth upstairs. Then he said, 'I picked you because of your shoes.' But I was wearing bad maroon Doc Martin knockoffs from Payless. I'm not sure if it was a line or not."

In the early 2000s, Ian Lobell was a frequent patron. "By then, it was seedy and rundown and a little tragic—for me, that only added to the appeal. I remember a deaf man who worked there. I had taken an ASL course, and one night, he did something that made me aware he was deaf or hard of hearing. So, I said something to him in sign language. He got so excited. He was so happy someone understood. We signed a little that evening, and we had a conversation after that whenever I saw him there."

Ron V went to the Bijou with a high school friend. A couple of years later, he returned on his own. "That was when I discovered the back patio and the upstairs. The dancers changed in what had to have been a janitor's closet. I'm not sure if they had lockers in there, but there were lockers at the bottom of the staircase for patrons who were going upstairs to check their clothes. You could bring your own lock or rent one at the front desk. The playroom upstairs drew a diverse crowd, very mixed and all ages. All these people together, no holds barred, just having fun. I saw a few, I don't want to call them straight, but couples who went there. Each time, they kept to themselves. One couple, in particular, drew a crowd at the spanking bench.

"Bijou workers sometimes walked through with flashlights but never bothered anybody. Nobody had much of an attitude there. The place was more welcoming than some places. There were a lot of men from out of town upstairs at the Bijou, a lot of guys in suits and ties. I saw a lot of wedding rings there."

"I lived way on the South Side," said Richard Kimmons, "and would commute all the way to the Bijou about once a week. At the Bijou, I learned sexual skills, the basics of glory hole etiquette, and how to reject someone politely. I went there more after I moved to the North Side, but by then the AIDS stuff was starting, so I pulled way back on my bookstore and Bijou behavior."

When AIDS hit Chicago, the Bijou remained in business despite the fact that sex clubs in other cities were shuttering. As Toushin explained, "...The city and the gay community got together and agreed that the bathhouses and places like the Bijou would be left alone. A lot of people came to the Bijou, so we were able to dispense AIDS information. We handed out condoms, put information up on the walls...a lot of information about AIDS and safe sex..." (de la Croix, 'Chicago Whispers #192,' *Windy City Times*).

In addition to safe sex literature, posters, and condoms, the Bijou had a safe sex announcement prior to the start of all the features. Toushin was quoted as saying, "I [now] only present films that have condom use. The only films I show that they are not used are the classic films from the pre-condom era. I make a distinction about this issue in my bareback policy."

In 1984, Steve Migalski turned 18. That year he attended his first Chicago Pride Parade. "I remember seeing the float for the Bijou Theater. After calling to hear that phone message all those years I decided to finally go see what it was all about. I got a fake ID and went. It was tantalizing and real, like stepping into something otherworldly. I was drawn to it and was there for probably four hours. The place also scared me. I didn't go back for three or four years."

Steve Marton ended many evenings at the Bijou. "We had a friend who lived in an apartment above. We came to his place and then went right to the second floor. That whole place blew my mind. The maze. Everything. I am not really into anything that intense in public, but I liked the idea of men meeting in this very dark place. You could hear whispers. Is it a connection? How far will the encounter go, and in what direction?"

"We called it 'The Beezh,'" said Brian Bouldrey, a Bijou patron from 1982 through 1985. "I remember how wild it was to see gay porn on the big screen. The theater at the Bijou was the dirtier part of the place. At least the upstairs got cleaned once in a while. The theater wasn't the same way. I remember kicking over a can of Coke and it started rolling towards the front of the theater, but it only rolled a little before it got stuck to the floor.

"Once, I was messing around with a guy in the theater, but we were looking for a little privacy. For some reason, we went behind this speaker in the front of the theater on the far left side of the stage. Once we got behind there, we let loose. The experience was so wild. We were doing this in the front of the theater, but it felt like we were in some secret place.

When I left the theater the guy at the desk said, 'Great show. Thanks again.'"

Boomer lived near the Bijou in the early 2000s. "I used to see guys going in there, but fewer over those years. I loved seeing the Bijou there—it was an anchor in the middle of all the gentrification happening along Wells St. The Bijou was there, still the same in the middle of all that change. I only went to the second floor a handful of times. It was seedy and never really clean. There was an element of danger. That was 90% of the fun."

"Today there's the Knob Hill (729 Bush St. in San Francisco, closed 2018), the Bijou, and I think there's a theater in New York (Kings Highway Cinema in Brooklyn, closed 2020)," said Toushin. "The world has changed, and you could now pick up an adult film in a bookstore or rent them in a video store, so the theater became like a dinosaur, there was no reason to go there to watch a movie." (de la Croix. 'Chicago Whispers #192,' *Windy City Times*).

"The Bijou was always entertaining," recalled Mark Hultmark. "With the theater, the bathroom, and the maze upstairs, you could always find what you were looking for."

Steve Migalski hadn't been to the Bijou in years when he returned with a friend in 2005. "That night we went to the Cell Block, Banana Video (4923 N. Clark, 2nd Fl.), and the Bijou. The upstairs at the Bijou was a labyrinth and it looked the same for the most part. That day, walking around, I thought, 'Oh my God. What have I been missing all these years?' It was great, but I didn't go back until the place was almost closing."

In 2008, the local paper/magazine *Newcity* wrote, "Walking into the Bijou...is much like walking into any other independent movie theater, the building smells musty, the seats are old, and most of the patrons are regulars. But since the Bijou Theater is attached to the longest-running sex club in the United States, the movies are gay porn, and the floors aren't sticky from popcorn." (Hieggelke. 'Sex You Up.' *Newcity*, 2008).

In 2011, the Bijou celebrated 40 years. For the 40th anniversary, Toushin promised a real shindig. "We are going to have some sexual street theater; strippers, we're making a short film history of the Bijou, blow up a few newspaper articles; bring in Bruno, a 1970 porn icon; have food and drink; serve a large cock cake that will have an orgasmic erupt; have giveaways, etc." (Forman, 'Bijou Marks 40 years of controversy.' *Windy City Times*, July 27, 2011).

Brian Dowling's 16-minute short film, *40 Years of Bijou,* tells the history of the theater and sex club from Toushin's perspective—how the theater went from an art house to a sex palace and his years in the business. Joining Toushin in the film is his friend, porn director Toby Ross, whose credits include *Cruisin' 57, School Mates,* and *California Boys.* Ross was a force in the 1970s and 1980s gay adult film world. Ross has been described as an important independent filmmaker who chose gay pornography as his focus.

Toushin took the occasion of the 40th anniversary of the theater to make a few remarks about the early decades of the Bijou. "The 1970s was the decade that followed Stonewall, [so] everything was an experiment, pushing boundaries, challenging society, new freedoms were demanded, nothing was given, everything was fought for... The 1980s was the decade that you demanded rights and demanded answers; the gay community wanted results. The 1980s was the era of life and death; you can't get anymore dramatic than that." (Forman, 'Bijou Marks 40 years of controversy.' *Windy City Times*, July 27, 2011).

A great deal had changed in the past 40 years. Bijou Video sales and distribution began in 1978. The second-floor playroom at the Bijou opened a bit after that. The status of the gay community in Chicago was also very different from what it was 40 years before. The last obscenity bust at the Bijou took place in 1991. The last raid of the theater by police was 15 years earlier, in 1996. However, some things at the Bijou remained constant.

"If the bars closed and I didn't get lucky, I went to the Bijou," said Screwdriver Joe. "Fridays and Saturday nights it was packed. 2 a.m. to 6 p.m. weekends were the busiest times upstairs. There were guys everywhere, leaning against the walls, posing, cruising, guys getting off. Those nights were a blur of dick."

"With safe sex and so much considered risky behavior, the Bijou was still nasty in the best way," recalled Jim P. "Upstairs was like a sex circus. You could be a part of things or you could watch. I mostly watched, but participated a little. I always got off."

'When I first came to Chicago from Detroit," said Mark Freitas, "There was a bartender at AA Meat Market (2933 N. Lincoln) named Teddy. He was also from Detroit. He had been in town a while and lived above the Bijou. We were a group of young gays that hung around him. For a Memorial Day cookout that Teddy had, we helped to set everything up and do the grilling so Teddy could host. Whenever we had parties at Teddy's, a few guys would sneak down to the second floor of the Bijou and explore. I never did."

"Some super-hot guys lived upstairs for a while," recalled Jiminez De Oaxaca. "And if you were hot and one of the guys was there, they took you upstairs. That was my goal for a while for whatever reason."

"I lived on the third floor above the Bijou for six months in 1983," said Jimmy D'Ambrosia. "It was when the song 'Beat It' by Michael Jackson was everywhere. There were two apartments on the 3rd floor that ran from front to back. I think it was the same on the 4th floor. The apartments were two bedrooms with a small kitchen and living room. There weren't many windows. You opened the door and stepped into the living room. About twenty feet ahead, the bathroom was on the right. On the left were the two bedrooms. The kitchen was straight ahead."

Joe W was a club kid in the early 1990s. "Sometimes I would go to Cairo (720 N. Wells St.) on Sundays for gay night and then go to after-hours parties. I went to parties a couple times in the apartments above the Bijou. Once my friend Mayday was there, and then disappeared. So, I went downstairs to see where Mayday had gone and just started exploring that whole second floor, which was wild—just a bunch of guys being naughty."

Brandon B lived above the Bijou as well. "Such a collection of characters lived in that building. We were all very cool about things. We had to be—after all, we were living above a gay porn theater. ...People would buzz our door at all hours thinking it was the buzzer for the Bijou and we would call down and say, 'Keep going, the buzzer is on your left.'"

In 2011, Steven Toushin told the *Windy City Times* that an estimated 5.5 million people had been to the Bijou over the last 40 years. He added, "The last five years, life at the Bijou has changed. The party is still here... it's just a little quieter.

"...There is nothing in the world like the Bijou. It is what sex was in the 1970s and '80s. The Bijou has never been pretty; it has always been deliciously nasty, and I'll keep it that way till I'm done, then I'll turn off the lights and go home." (Forman, 'Bijou Marks 40 years of controversy.' *Windy City Times*, July 27, 2011).

Three years later, in 2014, the Bijou was the venue to celebrate the release of Patrick Cowley's *School Daze* CD. Cowley (1950-1982) was a composer, producer, and pioneer of hi-NRG dance music. He redefined the genre by mixing psychedelic music and disco at a higher speed. His work was referred to as, "Masculine music for a new generation," meaning it was the gay fuck music of the future. Cowley's life was cut short just as his career began to flourish. He was part of the first wave of AIDS fatalities. Cowley died on November 12, 1982, at age 32.

A press release called the Valentine's Day release party for the *School Daze* CD a happening. "An intimate evening celebrating the life and times of one of history's most revered disco music producers. Join us as we transform America's oldest-running gay theater and sex club through multimedia art installations, live music, and adult performance in homage to Patrick Cowley and the newly released *School Daze* record."

Ivan Lozano moved to Chicago in 2009 for grad school. "I was fascinated at the time by the gay men who came before me and their cruising spaces. I was interested in seeing those places, so I explored them. I went to the Bijou a few times, but this was before PREP, so I wasn't as sexually free. Going there for me was more of an appreciation of the space and the graffiti that was on the walls and in the booths. I appreciated the way the light came in during the day when they opened the door to the back deck. That was when you could really see the graffiti—drawn dick and balls, phone numbers, meeting times—and cum stains all over the booths—it looked like decades of cum stains. I really wanted to photograph the space, but they were very protective of the clientele. Then, this opportunity to do an art installation with the Cowley music came up. It was a combined effort of the queer Chicago DJ group, the Men's Room, the Honey Sound System out of San Francisco, and Dark Entries Records, which was releasing the Cowley music.

"There were several different art installations for the event... My area of installation was the spiral staircase and the cluster of blowjob booths at the top of the stairs. I wanted to emphasize the cum stains and the graffiti. I did it by recreating the glory hole splatters and highlighting the cum stains with lighting. We visited the site and planned what we were

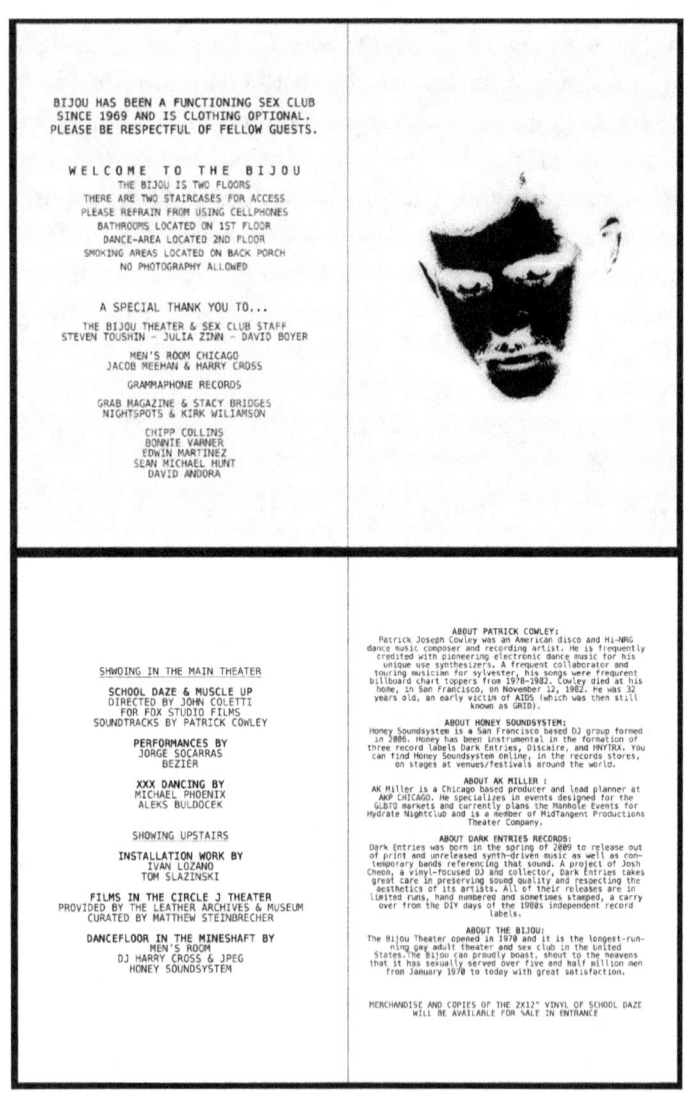

BIJOU HAS BEEN A FUNCTIONING SEX CLUB
SINCE 1969 AND IS CLOTHING OPTIONAL.
PLEASE BE RESPECTFUL OF FELLOW GUESTS.

WELCOME TO THE BIJOU
THE BIJOU IS TWO FLOORS
THERE ARE TWO STAIRCASES FOR ACCESS
PLEASE REFRAIN FROM USING CELLPHONES
BATHROOMS LOCATED ON 1ST FLOOR
DANCE-AREA LOCATED 2ND FLOOR
SMOKING AREAS LOCATED ON BACK PORCH
NO PHOTOGRAPHY ALLOWED

A SPECIAL THANK YOU TO...
THE BIJOU THEATER & SEX CLUB STAFF
STEVEN TOUSHIN - JULIA ZINN - DAVID BOYER

MEN'S ROOM CHICAGO
JACOB MEEHAN & HARRY CROSS

GRAMMAPHONE RECORDS

GRAB MAGAZINE & STACY BRIDGES
NIGHTSPOTS & KIRK WILIAMSON

CHIPP COLLINS
BONNIE VARNER
EDWIN MARTINEZ
SEAN MICHAEL HUNT
DAVID ANDORA

SHWOING IN THE MAIN THEATER

SCHOOL DAZE & MUSCLE UP
DIRECTED BY JOHN COLETTI
FOR FOX STUDIO FILMS
SOUNDTRACKS BY PATRICK COWLEY

PERFORMANCES BY
JORGE SOCARRAS
BEZIER

XXX DANCING BY
MICHAEL PHOENIX
ALEKS BULDOCEK

SHOWING UPSTAIRS

INSTALLATION WORK BY
IVAN LOZANO
TOM SLAZINSKI

FILMS IN THE CIRCLE J THEATER
PROVIDED BY THE LEATHER ARCHIVES & MUSEUM
CURATED BY MATTHEW STEINBRECHER

DANCEFLOOR IN THE MINESHAFT BY
MEN'S ROOM
DJ HARRY CROSS & JPEG
HONEY SOUNDSYSTEM

ABOUT PATRICK COWLEY:
Patrick Joseph Cowley was an American disco and Hi-NRG dance music composer and recording artist. He is frequently credited with pioneering electronic dance music for his unique use synthesizers. A frequent collaborator and touring musician for sylvester, his songs were frequent billboard chart toppers from 1978-1982. Cowley died at his home, in San Francisco, on November 12, 1982. He was 32 years old, an early victim of AIDS (which was then still known as GRID).

ABOUT HONEY SOUNDSYSTEM:
Honey Soundsystem is a San Francisco based DJ group formed in 2006. Honey has been instrumental in the formation of three record labels Dark Entries, Discaire, and HNYTRX. You can find Honey Soundsystem online, in the records stores, on stages at venues/festivals around the world.

ABOUT AK MILLER :
AK Miller is a Chicago based producer and lead planner at AKP CHICAGO. He specializes in events designed for the GLBTQ markets and currently plans the Manhole Events for Hydrate Nightclub and is a member of MidTangent Productions Theater Company.

ABOUT DARK ENTRIES RECORDS:
Dark Entries was born in the spring of 2009 to release out of print and unreleased synth-driven music as well as contemporary bands referencing that sound. A project of Josh Cheon, a vinyl-focused DJ and collector, Dark Entries takes great care in preserving sound quality and respecting the aesthetics of its artists. All of their releases are in limited runs, hand numbered and sometimes stamped, a carry over from the DIY days of the 1980s independent record labels.

ABOUT THE BIJOU:
The Bijou Theater opened in 1970 and it is the longest-running gay adult theater and sex club in the United States. The Bijou can proudly boast, shout to the heavens that it has sexually served over five and half million men from January 1970 to today with great satisfaction.

MERCHANDISE AND COPIES OF THE 2X12" VINYL OF SCHOOL DAZE WILL BE AVAILABLE FOR SALE IN ENTRANCE

The Patrick Cowley School Daze CD release party program at the Bijou, photo courtesy of Ivan Lozano.

going to do, but the installation itself happened the day of the event. We got there early and went to work. The doors for the party opened at 9 p.m. The place was packed that night and there were all sorts of queer party visuals. On the second-floor area in the back, beyond the chain link fence, was the dance floor and the DJs from Men's Room, Honey Sound System, and Dark Entries Records. All of them did DJ sets. Downstairs in the theater, there were performance artists on stage. ...Mostly, the Cowley event was about celebrating this queer space. It was bittersweet. The writing was on the wall for the Bijou. This space was not going to be around long."

Harry Cross did his first Men's Room party in 2012, "And we did the Men's Room show at the Bijou for a couple of years. I liked that we changed the music there a little. I mean, before that, it was sucking dick to Madonna's 'Lucky Star' and other pop stuff, and that's fine. We introduced some weirder things, like Patrick Cowley's music. I was happy when that influence was added to the cruising area. We had never done Men's Room in a space that large. That had challenges. The power would go out now and again, but it was just fusing trouble. The space was good for us. Men's Room was ready to grow the party. We set it up so the DJs were in the cage behind the chain link fence, and then people were dancing and playing outside the cage. We had speakers back in the booth area. I wanted someone to be back there sucking dick and thinking, 'This DJ is killing it.' For the vibe, we tried to make it not only electronic but sleazy disco as well—taking that cruisy down and dirty vibe and modernizing it into what cruisy down and dirty had become."

Mark Frietas appeared on the Bijou stage that evening as part of the queer hip-hop collective Banjee Report. "I played electronics while a DJ named Hijo Prodigo played tracks and I layered live parts over them. And Ace and Wallace would rap."

Derek da Silva was in charge of the BDSM performance on the stage at the Bijou that night, which featured bondage, fucking, and blood. "It was not just that, it was performance," offered da Silva, "but it was performance that included those elements. It was something that I don't think could have been done on stage anywhere else in the city."

"Downstairs we showed movies and had visual things on stage," recalled Harry Cross. "Around midnight, Banjee Report came on and did a show. Then Derek da Silva came out with a cock ring on his dick and balls with a chain hanging down and a disco ball at the end of the chain. Then he started to either poke himself with needles or cut himself because blood started to drip on the disco ball, and then they put a spotlight on this spinning bloody disco ball that was hanging from his balls. He always came up with something crazy and new, so when you were upstairs, and he came on, it was time to take the dick out of your mouth and go see the show."

A few months later, there was another Men's Room party at the Bijou; this one was presented by the Leather Archives and Museum (6418 N. Greenview Ave.) in a bash that went from 11:30 p.m. to 6 a.m. Music by Shaun J Wright, Juliana Huxtable, Harry & JPEG, Banjee Report, and once again featuring a BDSM performance by Derek da Silva. The flier read, "Ticket price includes entry, clothes check, beer and water; BJs, HJs, RJs, etc."

Richard H went to a Men's Room XXX Party at the Bijou over IML weekend in 2015. "Everyone was lined up outside to get in, so at 10 p.m. on Wells St., there were all these leather guys in jockstraps, chaps, and harnesses waiting for the party at the Bijou. The Bijou was in a very different neighborhood than it once was. Having us lined up on the sidewalk felt like a very 'clutch the pearls' kind of thing for the neighborhood. Inside, the Bijou had a red hue. Clearly, the space was derelict and hadn't been kept up. Some of the theater chairs were broken. The downstairs bathroom was bad. I'm not sure if we already knew it was closing later that year, but I remember part of wanting to go there was to check out this gay institution before it closed. I had read about gay porn theaters in the 1970s and 1980s, but it was before my time. So, when I was seeing that space and walking into the theater, part of me was saying, 'Oh, this is the sort of thing they were talking about.' It was a nice way to experience what older generations had experienced. Upstairs for the Men's Room XXX party, the first thing that hit me was the heat and the sexy, sweaty man odor. I saw the maze and the fuck stalls and the glory hole stalls; I saw Harry Cross behind the chain link fence and a lot of people dancing and carrying on."

The Bijou was celebrated as a space of sexual freedom, abandonment, and hedonistic joy, but there were other stories and layers happening simultaneously. When Ivan Lozano was setting up for the installation, he met a blind senior who came to the second floor of the Bijou every day. "Someone at the front desk walked him upstairs and he had his Subway sandwich. He sat there and ate and chatted with different people. I was so taken by the care that was given this man and that this sex place was his community."

Don Bell adds, "The Bijou was about more than sex. It was a gathering place for the community. It was important; it was a gathering place that centered around sexual orientation, and that was exciting and scary."

The Bijou was a place of sexual catharsis and awakening for Markt. "I had been married, and I went through a lot of issues with accepting that I was gay. While that was happening, I moved to Chicago. About the fifth time I went to the Bijou, I discovered the spiral staircase. Once I began having sex there, I realized I was attractive and good at sex. I used to love to go there, get off, and leave. It was a playground. There was a sense of brotherhood, camaraderie, a sense of people having sex and also having fun."

"The Bijou felt as though it had been there forever," said Richard F. "When it closed, it seemed the last of that sort of establishment was gone."

One September day in 2015, a note appeared on the Bijou door that read, "To all our Bijou customers. We have lost our lease. The end of days has come to the Bijou after 46 years."

Toushin elaborated to the *Windy City Times*, "The Bijou lost its lease at the longtime Wells St. location and was unable to move because its license was tied to the location. It's not the way I wanted to go out. I wanted to have a bit more time if I was going to close down after all these years." (Matt Simonette, 'Chicago's Bijou Theater to close Sept. 30.' *Windy City Times*, Sept. 11, 2015).

David Boyer threw the mammoth Bijou closing party on Sept. 28, 2015. The last full day of operation was September 29. After decades as part of Chicago gay nightlife, the doors of the Bijou Theater were locked for good at 9 a.m. on September 30, 2015.

Bijou owner Steven Toushin in front of the theater. Photo by Ross Forman, courtesy of Windy City Times.

To all our Bijou Customers

We have lost our lease

The END of DAYS has come to the BIJOU after 46 years.

Our last full 24 day in business will be Tuesday Sept 29th closing officially Wed. Sept 30 at 9 AM

The Bijou closing notification posted on the front door, courtesy Windy City Media Group.

The Glory Hole

When Bob Hugel decided to open a new gay bar at 1343 N. Wells St., he wanted to name the place the Glory Hole. Unfortunately, the Liquor Commission denied him the use of the name. Though the audacity of the proposed bar name on the application may have prompted gasps, Bob Hugel remained determined.

A Glory Hole advertisement depicting Mine #69, from Gay Life newspaper, courtesy of the Gerber Hart Library and Archives collection.

As the late David Cardwell explained, "The Liquor Commission had turned the name down. And he [Robert Hugel] wanted to know if he could do anything. ...[I] said, 'Well, you just tell him to tell them that [you are] naming it after the Glory Hole Mine in Central City, Colorado. That it is not a dirty word or anything.' There actually is a Glory Hole Mine in Central City, Colorado. ...He re-filed it and had all these explanations with it and the Liquor Commission bought it." (Jack Rinella Interviews, 1996).

And so, the Glory Hole Tavern opened on November 22, 1972—the day before Thanksgiving. Ads for the Glory Hole often referenced the bar's purported origin story with the dark opening of "Mine 69" prominently featured accompanied by a wooden signpost that read, "Enter At Your Own Risk." Beneath the image of the mineshaft was the bar tagline—"The Glory Hole, As Famous as its Name."

Sometimes ad copy for the Glory Hole took a different direction. "Looking for Adventure? Hot Men! Hot Music! Hot Dancing!" Prospects for getting lucky were good at the Glory Hole. The bar wasn't an out-and-out sex location, but it had an overtly sexual vibe combined with a good amount of "surprise sex and nudity." Much of the outrageousness that happened at the Glory Hole can be attributed to the free-flowing booze that helped to define the place.

Though considered a neighborhood bar, the Glory Hole was not a place that could be easily categorized. In 1976, the bar listings in *Gay Life* newspaper named three gay bars located along North Wells Street, each place was given a two-word description. Den One was a "dance bar." The Iron Butterfly (1437 N. Wells) was called a "western bar." And the two words used to describe the Glory Hole were "high camp."

The building that housed the Glory Hole resembled several buildings in the area, including the Bijou building. The Glory Hole was on the ground floor of a narrow four-story limestone building. There were two doorways on the face of the building. The doorway to the north was the entrance to the three apartments above the bar. South of this doorway was the three-paneled front window of the Glory Hole. The wooden window riser was filled with plants, obscuring the view inside. A drop-down shade was in place as well. To the right of the window was the entrance to the Glory Hole—up two well-worn steps to the door.

*Exterior of the Glory Hole Tavern, photo Ciao Magazine, Volume 2, Issue 2.
Courtesy of the Gerber Hart Library and Archives collection.*

"The Glory Hole had one of those gorgeous old hand-carved mahogany bars that practically ran the length of the place," recalled Allen Patrykus, "with an enormous antique mirror behind it."

Opposite the bar was a small stage for dancers. Beyond the bar was an area with a jukebox and a tiny dance floor, but people were known to dance on almost anything at the Glory Hole. To the side of the dance floor were two barrels that were drink holders but also used for dancing.

"I went to the Glory Hole before they had the pool. ...It used to get wild there," said Jim. "People would be playing with each other at the bar, fondling each other. They would have shows, and they used to have these wooden barrels that guys used to dance on. I remember...the Ringo Starr song 'Devil Woman' (1973) came out and I got up on one of the barrels, and this guy got up on the other, and we were dancing and taking off our clothes, or whatever. I got down to my underwear, and at the end of the song, at the exact end, the barrel broke, and I fell through it. They said it was like those old-fashioned shows, where you have no clothes, just the barrel with the straps. I had nothing on except underwear, and the barrel covered that..." (de la Croix, 'Chicago Whispers, #217,' *Windy City Times*).

"The space was long and high ceilinged," said Bob M. "But mostly, I remember it had a sleazy feel that, even during the day, sex might just happen. That's a good thing. Smoking was still allowed in bars and I could smoke there, but even for a smoker, the place was smoky."

"The Glory Hole reminded me of the New Flight (420 N. Clark St.)—A gay bar with a lot of younger guys and older men," added Frank Nichter. "The place smelled like stale beer and cigarettes, and it had a sleazy reputation. I went there quite a bit."

"I worked there, lived there, and screwed there. I might have never left the block if it wasn't to go to the Gold Coast and the Bistro," laughed Race Bannon. "I bartended on and off at the Glory Hole between 1973 and 1977. I was boinking Bob, the owner, at the time. I was 18 when I started working there. I moved in upstairs with Bob and his lover, Paul. My room looked down onto the backyard area of the bar. Beautifying the back patio was one of Bob's pet projects. He wanted to do different things, and since he lived there too, the back area was part of his home. He got a pool. He saw the pool as a draw for the bar and something unique, something no other bar had at the time. The pool was pretty busy during the summer months. It was set all the way back on the property against the fence by the alley."

The five-foot above-ground backyard pool, the sort with no filter that takes a day to fill with a garden hose, stood behind the Glory Hole for years. After Den One opened in 1974, the 1300 block of North Wells had a gay bar with an indoor pool (Den One) as well as the Glory Hole with an outdoor pool.

Richard T recalled, "[The Glory Hole] had go-go boys and a marvelous patio with an above-ground pool where patrons would shuck their clothes and cool off on hot summer nights. The signature touch, though, was the two signs flanking the patio doors: Keep Off the Grass (there was nothing resembling grass beyond the doors), and No Dogs Allowed (the owner's poodle and current litter were always underfoot out there)." (de la Croix, 'Chicago Whispers #138,' *Chicago Outlines*).

The Glory Hole speedos with the bulls-eye butt being modeled at the Belmont Rocks, courtesy of Gay Chicago, 1976.

"Bob and Jeff had six dogs when I was living there," added Bannon. "Two Standard Poodles, a German Shepherd, two Chihuahuas, and a Shepoodle—the Shepherd bred with one of the Poodles. Those dogs had free reign of the place and were always running around that back patio area where the pool was, even when there was a barbeque."

Folks could wear whatever they wanted in the pool—cutoffs, underwear, or nothing at all. In 1976, the Glory Hole launched their signature bar speedos. The Glory Hole swimsuits were red with "the Glory Hole" written in a circle on the butt. The circle on the ass had the visual effect of being a bulls-eye. The bar had the speedos for sale while supplies lasted. Many were given as prizes in the bar in the months that followed.

The grand reopening of the Glory Hole beer garden usually coincided with Mother's Day. In 1977, the celebration was larger and a bit more grand than usual. That year, the redesign of the back patio area, including the reopening of the pool, was unveiled. As an added draw, the invitations for the party promised, "An inaugural performance of the Glory Hole Water Follies at dusk."

Gay Life columnist Ron Helizon did a piece on bars with back patios in 1979. Prominently featured in his rundown was the Glory Hole. "Enjoy lush tropical plants and flowers, let the trees shade you, or sun yourself on the deck at the Norma Desmond swimming pool..."

"The Glory Hole was known for having the best beer garden," added Allen Patrykus. "It was beautiful back there with different paths and plantings and seating areas. The apartments above had flowerpots on the back steps, and ferns and vines were dripping from the porch railings. There was a pool, but people were usually having sex in there. People were having sex all over back there."

"That back patio was nice," explained Dean Ogren. "I liked going there in the summer and sitting outside or in the pool and having cocktails with friends—maybe smoke some weed, plenty of that going on back there."

"It didn't feel like a bar back there, it felt like a party in someone's backyard," offered Jim P.

"Once about six or eight of us were out and ended up there, and we got naked and hopped in that pool and started having chicken fights and everything," recalled Del B.

"They were one of the first places to open an outdoor patio, and the owner decided to put in a pool," recalled Wally. "If you got there the day they changed the water, you were ok. Any time after that...I mean, things would float on the top of the water there. This is no BS, things would actually float." (de la Croix, 'Chicago Whispers #207, *Windy City Times*).

"Once, I went there with a friend," recalled Frank Nichter. "We had been out a while, and we were loaded. Anyway, we stripped down to our underwear and hopped in the pool. So we're having a good time and splashing, and all of a sudden, I looked, and there was a turd right there. So, I screamed, and I mean screamed, 'Oh my God, there's a turd in the swimming pool!' We got out of the pool very fast, but we didn't leave. We just got dressed and continued to party."

The Glory Hole had a couple of pinball machines in the back by the restroom. Terence Alan Smith, aka Joan Jett Blakk, liked to go there after taking MDA to play pinball. "The Glory Hole had three different flipper pinball machines. Once, we bought what we thought was MDA, but was really Angel Dust. Three of us took it, and we all had different experiences. That was the night I got the chip in my front tooth. I was running around tripping on Angel Dust behind the Glory Hole and fell down by the pool. Something I loved about that bar and having that pool in the back was that I have a fetish for feet, and a bar with a pool meant that you saw men's feet all the time."

Pool parties at the Glory Hole sometimes included several additional inflatable kiddie pools. JC called the Glory Hole the wildest place of all. "We had orgies out in the back. They had a couple of dogs there who had puppies. People would say, 'Oh, let's go see the puppies.' Then they'd be fooling around back there in the bushes." (de la Croix, 'Chicago Whispers #223,' *Windy City Times*).

"It was a hard-drinking place," recalled Daniel L. "People had sex sometimes in the back garden by the pool. I remember seeing it and thinking, 'People get into that pool?' I would go to the Glory Hole late at night sometimes—as a 4 a.m. bar, it was a place to go for one more cocktail, one more chance to meet someone."

"You could lock the bathroom door at one time," said Jim L, "but the other part of the hook (the eyelet) was out of the wood. So, the bathroom had a hook, but it didn't lock."

"The Glory Hole felt like hanging out with family," said Race Bannon, "People would drop by for a drink or to chat on their way home from work or before heading out for the evening. Tips were great. I was a former gymnast and dancer. When I bartended there, I wore hot pants. I knew how to make money. We had Rush poppers behind the bar. The tips were all cash. I could walk out at the end of the night with $100-150 in 1970s dollars.

"One day, Bob introduced me to a man who had dropped out of the seminary before taking his final vows. When he introduced him, Bob said something like, 'This is the kind of guy you should be with.' He was right. Kevin moved in with me upstairs and we both lived with Bob and his partner. I was with Kevin Lockwood for 14 years until he died."

"I've always liked guys in Levi's and a beard," said Allen Patrykus. "And there were plenty of working-class guys at the Glory Hole—that was right up my alley. The Glory Hole poured a good cocktail, but I also saw them serve the drunkest people. The Glory Hole never cut people off."

"I remember being there and thinking, this is the last stop before AA," recalled Steve Lutz. "Lots of heavy drinkers, and I was one of them. The Glory Hole was a friendly neighborhood bar that was intense sometimes, mostly because of the crazy amount of alcohol consumed. Once, I went there after work and started drinking. A couple of hours later, I was passed out at the bar. I came to a half hour later. I asked the bartender if I passed out, and he said that I did, but since I wasn't bothering anyone, he just let me be. I was mortified that people had been there and seen me passed out at the bar. That describes the place well. The Glory Hole was the sort of place where you could pass out at the bar, and as long as you weren't bothering anyone, they let you be."

"The Glory Hole was friendly and wild," added Mark Hultmark. "Expect anything when you went there. All kinds of stuff—guys sitting at the bar with their dicks out, anything and everything."

"Bob had the Glory Hole, but he had plans for a second, more upscale place," offered Race Bannon. "He was going to call it Sutter's Mill." The name was a continuation of the prospecting theme that Hugel started with the Glory Hole. When gold was discovered at Sutter's Mill in 1848, the find sparked the California Gold Rush.

Hugel was eager to open a second place. He had even gone so far as to take over a former candy shop to convert it into Sutter's Mill. Bannon explained, "Bob purchased a candy store with everything inside, so we learned to make giant lollipops and pour the candy into the mold. We made all that stuff and tried to sell off as much of it as we could."

In the end, Sutter's Mill never happened, but the party continued at the Glory Hole.

On December 31, 1976, the Glory Hole had a Piss on '76 Party. Ad copy for the shindig read, "See the New Year's baby (matured beyond his years) give the Bi-Centennial baby his 'dew.' Free bubbly when the cock strikes midnight! Come early, stay late. Tickets good for 2 free drinks til noon on New Year's Day will be issued between midnight and 4 a.m. New Year's Day, the orgy continues at 7 a.m. Cash in your drink tickets to enter the New Year's Baby competition—bring a diaper and a shoulder banner bearing the year of your birth to compete for a $50 cash prize. Judging at 8 p.m."

Joey McDonald went to the Glory Hole the day he turned 21. "It was 1976. I wore my navy uniform. I remember getting drunk and doing a strip tease on the bar. I remember the plaster penis that hung above the bar there was huge—I am guessing 4-5 feet long. That night, I picked up a couple of guys, and they promptly took me to Man's Country."

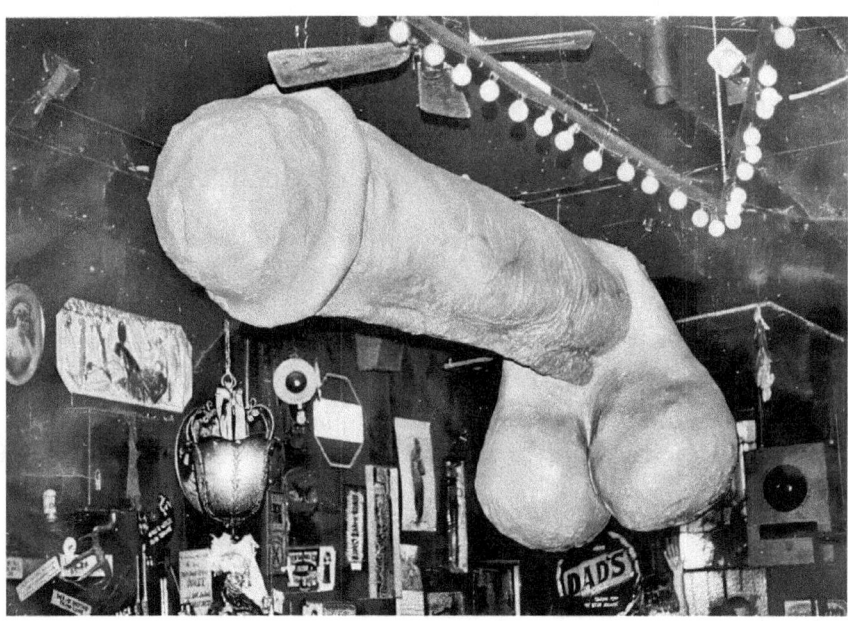

The giant penis that hung for a while above the bar at the Glory Hole Tavern. Photo courtesy of the Leather Archives and Museum.

Malone Sizelove remembers the plaster penis that hung over the bar at the Glory Hole, "During the holidays, they put Christmas lights on it." The enormous plaster penis and balls were a sporadic decoration at the Glory Hole, but the fate of the giant cock and balls remains a mystery.

Was the giant penis destroyed or damaged beyond repair? By all accounts, the Glory Hole clientele loved the big cock and balls.

Brian D Smith said, "The Glory Hole was one of those places you went to if you wanted to feel naughty. It was very easy to get laid there."

"I could tell it was a fun place as soon as we stepped inside," said Tay. "The floor was sticky from all the spilled beer and there were strippers on the bar."

"The Glory Hole was one of those places. When you went there, you brought the smell of the bar home with you," said Terence Alan Smith, "Cigarettes, stale beer, the evening... That bar marked you."

"Mysterious Marilynn tended bar briefly at the Glory Hole," added Allen Patrykus. "When they eventually fired her, she threw a bottle and smashed that big, beautiful mirror that was behind the bar. I met Marilynn at Carol in Exile. She was in the shows there. We became roommates. For her drag, Mysterious Marilynn acted out her version of the song with props. When she did 'Wasted' by Donna Summer, Marilynn pulled out a bag of talcum powder and pretended to do lines. When Richard and I got together, and Mother Carol told him to keep me away from the 'drug people'—Mysterious Marilynn was one of the people she meant."

"Friends and I used to come up from St. Louis," offered Rick Garcia. "We'd go to a couple other bars and then the Glory Hole. Who knows what they thought of us? There were usually three or four of us, and we would show up with our hair sprayed and wearing lipstick and bronzer in our platform shoes and Qiana shirts. I saw the pool, and at the time, I thought, 'I would rather walk through the sewers of the city than get into that thing.' Every time we went there, they tried to get us to dance— alone, with other guys, anything. The answer was always, 'No. Absolutely not.' We were insufferable. I'm sure they just groaned when they saw us walk in."

Go-go boys were a constant at the Glory Hole. The dancers there tended to be young and slender gay guys, twinks. The stage was across from the bar, but at the Glory Hole, the dancers often performed on the bar instead.

Steve "Missie" Allmann added, "I remember one time when this guy, who used to dance with a snake, fell off the stage. His snake had got loose and was crawling away. He was trying to catch it." (de la Croix, 'Chicago Whispers #226, *Windy City Times*).

Robert Link and his pet boa, Shleena, are mentioned in the Karlin and de la Croix book, *Last Call*. "In June 1984, vice officers and a television crew burst into the bar. Six men were arrested. The State's Attorney decided not to proceed with the charges. However, one of the dancers received 30 days of court supervision for exposing his genitals. ...In another raid in June 1985, Tactical officer Terry Pekara claimed that Robert Link, a dancer, used his snake, Shleena, in an obscene manner."

"I remember him. When he danced with the snake, the boa would coil around his naked body, including his cock," added Brian D Smith.

Robert Kimmons was at Carol's when someone asked if he'd seen the stripper with a snake. "I hadn't seen that. So, we walked down to the Glory Hole and sure enough, he was on stage dancing. Everybody there was fascinated by him and cautious when tipping. When I asked if I could pet his snake, he asked, 'Which one?' I said, 'The one around your neck.' The snake was so calm that I ended up talking to him about it. He told me that he made sure to give the snake a big meal before he had to work."

"At the Glory Hole, people just sometimes sucked dick in the bar," recalled Race Bannon. "People did a lot in bars back then. I remember bartending and the owner, Bob, being right there, and he was not too upset if a dancer was getting a blowjob."

"The Glory Hole had unofficial nude dancing," said David Plomin. "That's why everyone went there. The dancers did not only flash it for that brief time before the end of their set, but suddenly, everything was off, and you'd go, 'Oh my god, are the cops going to come in?'"

As Screwdriver Joe put it, "The Glory Hole was a very friendly bar that gave the customers what they wanted."

"The Glory Hole was the first gay bar I went in," recalled Jimmy D'Ambrosia. "At the time, I thought it smelled stale. Now, I recognize the smell as beer and poppers. There was a dancer on the bar wearing a ribbed white jockstrap, only the white was kind of gray."

"The strippers there were very friendly working for their tips," recalled Steve Lutz. "I was a tipper, so they got friendly with me, but I went more for men than for twinks. And the dancers at the Glory Hole tended to be twinks."

"In 1980, I went there with a friend of mine. We were drinking and they convinced me to get on stage and start dancing," said Tigg. "The guy who owned the bar offered me a job. The stage there was more like a shelf—no more than 6' x 4' and guys would put their drinks on that too. Sometimes, there were even two of us on the stage at the same time, but then all we could do was sort of bump and grind on each other."

Chris G thought the name of the place was hilarious. "And they had strippers. Not many gay bars had dancers at the time. In the mid-1980s, the next closest place was probably the Inner Circle (2546 N. Clark). I enjoy watching sexy men dance, so the Glory Hole was perfect."

Malone Sizelove remembered the bar periodically showing vintage 16mm porn with no sound. "But my main attraction there were the Latino dancers."

Mercury and his brother went to the Glory Hole in the late 1970s for the $1.25 pitchers of beer. "We were sitting there, and I watched this dancer get up and make good money in 15 minutes. I thought, 'What is this magic?' Then, the owner offered me $25 to dance for 15 minutes. I told him I didn't have anything to wear, and he opened two drawers behind the bar filled with G-strings. I made good money that night. The Glory Hole was where I realized how much money dancing could bring in compared to my wage for 40 hours a week."

Around 1980, Screwdriver Joe frequented the Glory Hole with a friend. "Jose used to love to go there and get up on things and dance. He loved showing off. My job was to make sure nobody jumped up there with him or tried to pull him down. As far as I remember, no one told him to get down or anything."

To strip at the Glory Hole, Tigg wore short shorts and a G-string. "I had a special tuxedo one and another that was an anteater. One time, a guy put a roll of quarters inside it, and everything fell off from the weight—so I was dancing naked for a while, but my tips went way up after that."

"I danced there about six months," said Dean Ogren. "When I was there all of us dancers looked like we could have used a hamburger. When I was at the Glory Hole there was no DJ, so dancing there meant we were at the mercy of whatever somebody put on the jukebox—and it wasn't all disco or dance stuff. It was hard trying to do a sexy strip to Liza Minnelli's 'Cabaret' or 'New York, New York' or some other things they would play there. It paid $25 a night. I drank free and kept the tips."

"When we got there, even if they were ready to close, they let us in," recalled Jean. "They were fine having a woman there, especially since I was with a group of gay guys, plus we were good tippers. We engaged in plenty of debauchery there. We would drink and laugh and drink and laugh, and because of all that partying, I grew comfortable hanging around a lot of gay men. That was how I got into bartending at gay bars."

The Glory Hole played an unexpected part in Michael Kramer's coming out story. "My dad worked for a jeweler downtown. He was a quiet man from the suburbs, but he worked with a man who was a part owner of the Glory Hole or something. This guy would come into work and regale my dad with these tales of what happened at the Glory Hole over the weekend. In 1981, I came out to my father. When I told him, he said, 'I wondered when you were going to say something.' He was very cool with it, but then he said, 'My advice to you is, don't be too kinky.' After that talk, I remember wondering what my dad meant by that. What does my father know? It turned out his coworker's tales of the Glory Hole were all he had to go on as to what gay life was."

"The Glory Hole showed a lot of movies," recalled Race Bannon. "Bob's secret desire was to open a vintage movie theater. Movies were shown on a pull-down screen in the front window area. When I was there, we must have shown *The Rocky Horror Picture Show* 16 times, and every time we showed the movie, it drew a crowd."

The Glory Hole movie times were Wednesday nights at 10:30 and Saturday afternoons at 4:00. The featured films were an eclectic mix— *Hollywood Canteen, Shine on Harvest Moon, Kentucky Fried Movie, The Many Adventures of Winnie the Pooh, West Side Story, Easter Parade, Life with Father, Alice's Restaurant, The Sting, Charade, the Magical Voyage of Sinbad, The 12 Chairs, Night of the Living Dead, Meet Me in St. Louis, Rollerball, Lords of Flatbush, Thoroughly Modern Millie, The Boys in the Band, The Producers, The Horn Blows at Midnight, Cat Ballou, Where's Poppa?, Gypsy, Charlie's Aunt, Magical Mystery Tour,* and *Flesh Gordon,* the X-rated straight soft-core parody of the space film serial. During each feature, the bar served plenty of salted popcorn.

The Glory Hole showings sometimes had themes. October meant a horror fest featuring a different chiller each week. One year the lineup was *Count Yorga, Vampire* (1970), Vincent Price in *The Conqueror Worm*, *Count Dracula* with Christopher Lee, and the Helmut Berger version of *The Picture of Dorian Gray*. Following the death of choreographer and director Busby Berkeley in March of 1976, the Glory Hole paid tribute to his genius with a mini film festival featuring several of his musical extravaganzas—*Dames, Goldiggers in Paris, Goldiggers of 1935, Goldiggers of 1937, Wonder Bar*, and *Fashions of 1934*.

Attending a Sunday film showing also meant attending the Glory Hole Sunday barbecue from 4 p.m. to 9 p.m. on the back patio, weather permitting. Sometimes, the parties in the garden required more space. On special occasions, the Glory Hole teamed up with the Bijou and Carol's Speakeasy to have interconnected backyard parties.

"When they opened things up," said Jaime Krohn, "You could go from the back of the Glory Hole behind the Bijou to the back of Carol's—all of that. They had parties where they opened it all up. The back area was all connected."

One year in the heat of summer, the Glory Hole, the Bijou, and Carol's Speakeasy hosted the Emperor Strikes Back Party. Patrons were welcome to move freely from the Glory Hole to the Bijou to Carol's. For the collaborative summertime party, each business offered something extra. At the Glory Hole, the party began at 8 p.m. in the Roman garden, as the back area was christened for the night. Print advertisements for the party read, "Come see our hanging Roman garden & our hung male dancers!"

Don't miss out on the bacchanal!

At 10 p.m., the Glory Hole had a show featuring performances by popular drag artists Ginger Grant and Diana Hutton. Grant (d. 2018) became a longtime performer and emcee at the Baton Show Lounge as well as the first Miss Continental Plus in 1991. The late Diana Hutton performed around Chicago and was in the cast at the show bar La Cage (50 East Oak St.) before relocating to Nashville. She went on to become Miss Gay US of A in 1987.

For the Emperor Strikes Back party, the Glory Hole pool was kept open all night long. For the party, the back patio at the Bijou featured the lovely gardens as well as a few outdoor booths, most of them with glory holes. Walking north, the next back area was Carol's. At the Speakeasy there were drink specials and a midnight drag show featuring Hedda Lettuce, Diana Hutton (again), Jan Howard, Cotton Candy, and Emperor Steve.

The Glory Hole was big on theme parties. The bar transformed into Berlin for Oktoberfest, or at least the Glory Hole version of Berlin. "Grab your lederhosen and come get a juicy sausage!" On the back patio of the Glory Hole was a full spread of German food. For Oktoberfest, the Glory Hole strippers became, "Our dancing German beauties."

In June 1979, the Village People released two albums, *Go West* and *Live and Sleazy*. They also appeared at the Aragon Ballroom. To celebrate the phenomenal success of the disco group, the Glory Hole held a four-day Village People celebration with added contests. Dressing as one of the iconic Village People "types" meant free drinks and eligibility for special prizes. The six types that comprised the concept group were a policeman, a construction worker, a leatherman, a Native American, a cowboy, and a soldier. A *Gay Life* newspaper ad promoting the Glory Hole event read, "Come on down and express the 'village' in you. It's our 7th year, and we're still here. Perhaps the most 'village' bar in Chicago."

Though event and theme nights were relatively frequent at the Glory Hole, no special occasion was required for a memorable evening. "One night, there was a beer fight in that bar, and everybody was just soaked," said JC. "I think it was started by one of our girlfriends who used to come over there with us...All I remember was I got drenched with beer. All of a sudden, everyone was shooting beer at each other, and we came out of there drenched." (de la Croix, 'Chicago Whispers #223,' *Windy City Times*).

The Trim the Hole Party at the Glory Hole was a holiday crafting party. The event was a week after Thanksgiving, on December 1, 1977. Ad copy read, "Tis the season to be jolly! Don't wait for St. Nick. Be an elf. Be yourself. Enjoy your favorites—Christmas goodies, cookies, candies, a party, and a pear tree. Come decorate—Hang your balls at the Glory Hole. Win a bottle of Christmas Cheer. Don't forget. Don we now our gay apparel." Crafting that night included making decorations as well as a cock-sock decorating contest with a fashion parade following. Cash prizes for cock-sock crafting were given to those entrants with the Biggest, Most Original, and Best S&M cock socks.

Glory Hole advertisement, courtesy of Gay Chicago.

The Wet Jockey Shorts Dance Contest became a Glory Hole fixture. The winner of every Tuesday contest received $25. The weekly winners then competed in a runoff contest every six weeks. The winner of the runoff contest was awarded a cash prize of $100. The contest had 'celebrity' judges as an additional draw. Mother Carol was a judge in one of the runoff contests, as were Roby Landers and Michael K.

Roby Landers (1931-1978) was a drag legend and a major influence in the development of the Chicago show bar scene of the 1960s and 1970s. Her first local gig of note was as stage manager/headliner at the

Some action on the Glory Hole back patio, photo courtesy of Drummer Magazine V5, #38, 1982. From the Leather Archives and Museum collection.

Chesterfield (2831 N. Clark) in the mid-1960s. In the early 1970s, Landers became stage manager and headliner at Sparrows (5224 N. Sheridan). In the mid-1970s, Landers opened her own club where she was owner, stage manager, and headliner. House of Landers (936 W. Diversey Pkwy) was a show lounge on two levels beside the Brown Line elevated train. Landers eventually moved to Atlanta, where she was performing and working as a dressmaker when she died of a heart ailment in June 1978.

In 1978, *Gay Life* reported that Wanda Lust hosted the Mr. Go-Go Boy Contest at the Glory Hole and that Wanda had "Many in the room rolling on the floor." Wanda Lust (1944-1980) was the drag hostess and stage manager of the Music Hall at the bathhouse, Man's Country. In addition, Wanda was a gay men's sexual health activist and a popular nightlife personality who always had a gig somewhere around town. Wanda even tended bar at the Glory Hole periodically, not in drag, but as Stephen Jones.

In 1982, leather and kink magazine *Drummer* wrote, "For some nine years now, the Glory Hole has been one of Chicago's sturdiest

The Glory Hole float from the 1976 Chicago Pride Parade, photo courtesy of Gay Chicago.

neighborhood-and-more bars. The crowd, particularly on weekends, is a fun collection of varying degrees of leather and Levi sorts. The bar's 'laissez-faire' attitude towards its patrons makes this one of the city's most relaxed watering holes.

"Relaxed, but far from sleepy! On Sunday afternoons, the garden out back of the Glory Hole hops with all kinds of hot action covering the benches and tables. And during the summer, the pool in the garden (a feature unique to Chicago) is usually surrounded with sweat glistening no-tan-line sunbathers. The fence and trees provide the privacy; the men provide the action.

"The dance floor is gone (it was too small anyway), but the music plays on (heavy on the rock). And so does the partying—The Glory Hole is one laid back 'let's party' bar. Take advantage of it." (*Drummer Magazine* #38, 1982.)

Despite the air of frivolity, there were serious doings going on at the bar. The Glory Hole was one of the four bars to testify against the mob in the 1980s. The *Chicago Tribune* reported that the mafia used "threats of force and violence and threats of economic harm to extract payments from the victims." The other three bars to testify were Carol's Speakeasy, and two Jim Flint establishments, the Redoubt and the Baton Show Lounge. (Rudolph Unger, 'Two mobsters indicted in tavern shakedowns.' *Chicago Tribune*, Dec. 9, 1983).

The following synopsis of events is from *Jim Flint: The Boy From Peoria*. "Bob Hugel testified that in November 1978, one of his employees passed on a note left for him. He was to "get in touch with Johnny at Carton's Restaurant (21 E. Chestnut). Shaken, he spoke with Mother Carol about it. His anxiety mounting, Hugel contacted the FBI. After meeting with officials, he gave them the note and agreed to cooperate with authorities.

"Two days later, Hugel returned to Carton's Restaurant to meet Johnny—this time wearing a recording device and with FBI agents nearby. The tape from that day was played at the trial. "Listen, you know we got an association here in the district, you understand? You're not a member of the association, you got to come in.' Hugel was asked for $400 a month. When he complained, the amount was lowered to $300.

"The following day, Hugel brought $200 of FBI cash. On tape: 'Listen, it's not that bad, 'cause the other guys are rougher than I am, you know what I mean, they're dirty mother-fuckers.' When Hugel voiced his fears, he was met with, 'Nothing to be afraid of. You understand? ... Don't worry about it, you hear? Give me the hundred, gotta have the hundred before the 10th, alright?'

"Hugel, the owner of the Glory Hole from 1972-1979, testified that he feared for himself and his business. For the $300 a month, Hugel said he expected, 'For them to leave me alone.' He claimed he did not want to pay the money. He expected no services in exchange for the payment and that he did not need protection.

"After testifying at the mafia trial, Hugel went into federal witness protection. The indictments were announced in December 1983 with the trial scheduled for the following September 1984." (Baim, Keehnen, *Jim Flint: The Boy From Peoria.* Prairie Avenue Productions, 2011.)

By the mid-to-late 1980s, the days of free-flowing booze and unbridled debauchery that helped to define bars like the Glory Hole were rapidly becoming a thing of the past as AIDS took hold in the city. With the advent of AIDS, nightlife changed. Folks began to curtail their partying and carousing. For many, the change came too late. A solid percentage of the patrons who filled the barstools at the Glory Hole were now growing ill and dying.

The Glory Hole shut off the lights and locked the doors for good on April 29, 1988.

Arcades:
The Over 21 Bookstore
& The Peeping Tom

Though their numbers plummeted with the advent of online porn, for decades adult bookstores and arcades were a key part of the sexual landscape. The *Chicago Tribune* reported in 1977 that there were 57 adult bookstores in Chicago. The list of adult bookstores, including the name of the owner, was compiled by "the city council's special subcommittee on obscenity." ('List of 57 porn bookstores compiled by city council panel.' *Chicago Tribune*, July 7, 1977)

The sign over the sidewalk at the entrance to the Over 21 Bookstore, photo by John O.

A significant percentage of these bookstores/arcades catered to gay men who saw adult bookstores as another place to play, get off, and explore their sexuality. The arcades and porn video shops were a common sight in Old Town, with at least five arcades, not including the Bijou, on the four-city-block stretch of Wells between Division Street and North Avenue. Two adult arcades were on the 1300 block—the Over 21 Bookstore at 1347 N. Wells and the Peeping Tom at 1345 N. Wells. Two additional bookstores, also listed in the *Chicago Tribune* piece, were the Swinging Times Adult Bookstore at 1403 N. Wells and Wells News, Inc. at 1520 N. Wells.

As video arcades became more commonplace in the 1970s, adult bookstores became sex destinations instead of adult product retailers. Most bookstores and arcades, especially those catering to a gay clientele, no longer paid the rent with the sale of skin magazines and "adult-only" novels. The moneymaker was the arcade, especially if some of the booths had glory holes. Typically, admittance to the arcade was a separate admission fee. The transaction often included the purchase of tokens or change for quarters to feed the projectors. Some arcades had attendants—if the door to a booth was closed, the movie had stopped, and the projector wasn't being fed—they knocked.

As the owner of two arcades near his leather bar, the Gold Coast (501 N. Clark St.), Chuck Renslow (1929-2017) offered some insights into the business at the time. Renslow opened the Machine Shop at 510 N. Clark as well as a second bookstore and arcade, the Tool Box, at 414 N. Clark. At the Tool Box, instead of a slab of particleboard or paneling between the booths, some had Plexiglas.

Running the arcades, especially before VHS, is tough to imagine today. Renslow called his place the Machine Shop because "There were so many damn machines in it." Each booth had its own projector and each projector needed to be plugged in—and some booths had more than one feature option—so imagine the number of cords, plugs, and wires required for a place like the Machine Shop, which advertised as having "the most arcade booths in Chicago." In 1984, the Machine Shop followed the ongoing migration to the Lakeview neighborhood, relocating to 3704 N. Halsted.

Descriptions of gay adult arcades are often a blend of grit and glory—profane with shades of the sacred. The similarities are there—the dim light, a distinctive scent, and sounds that enhance the quiet. In an adult bookstore those sounds were whispers, the scuff of pacing feet, a projector's whirr, creaking partitions, and the muffled, or not muffled, sounds of sex.

In his novel *Some Dance to Remember* (2005), Jack Fritscher wrote, "The baths and arcades teach homomasculinism. In their mazes, men cruise to find reflections of their preferences. More than one Telemachus searches for his daddy and finds him. More than one Narcissus seeks himself and gladly, madly, drowns in all his reflections. More than one Odysseus looks from cave door to cave door for his young sailing companions. David puts his arms around his Jonathan. Walt Whitman finally sees the night that men of his predilection embrace one another with muscular arms, unembarrassed, in public places. Butch fucks Sundance. Recruits stiffen before the hard-jawed commands of their ultimate Drill Instructor. Nasty bikers kneel to suck off the greasy Wild One. Jocks wrestle with golden champions. Leathermen submit to the rope-tying midnight cowboy who smokes like the Marlboro Man and sits his sweet dingleberry pucker down smack on their faces. Tennessee Williams was right: 'Sometimes there's God so quickly, so... suddenly... so last summer.'"

Fritscher also addresses the subject in chapter three of *Popular Witchcraft* (2004). In the book, Fritscher writes, "According to the dogma of Saint Priapus, gay anonymous sex is fundamental priapic worship. A particularly popular 'kneeling' ritual is anonymous fellatio, performed through 'glory holes' cut in walls of confessional-like booths, through which the penis alone 'appears' as if disconnected from the body on the other side of the wall.

"Catholics once venerated a more modest Saint Priapus, until the Second Vatican Council in 1964 purged him and dozens of other "saints," some of whom, like Priapus, were pagan demi-Gods who had crept into Catholic devotions on their own tiptoes while Christianity was busy appropriating other bits it chose from paganism."

In the summer of 1969, a fire on North Wells Street caused severe damage to Big Dean's hot dog grill at 1347 N. Wells St. "A crowd estimated at several hundred persons last night watched 70 firemen and 14 pieces of equipment battle a fire which damaged the rear of three buildings in Old Town." The blaze also spread to the rear of the buildings on either side—the Purple Cow, a bar, at 1347 N. Wells St., and the Candy Barrel at 1345 N. Wells. ('North Side Fire.' *Chicago Tribune,* June 17, 1969).

In 1971, the "world famous" Over 21 Bookstore opened in the vacated space at 1347 N. Wells St. The facade of the Over 21 was painted black, which only enhanced the vibrant yellow signage that was highlighted by naked marquee bulbs. Above the doorway was another illuminated sign, Adult Movies .25 cents per play. On one side of the doorway was a vibrant yellow sign, Adult Reading. Adult Movies. The south exterior wall was also painted black with a circular yellow sign, Over 21 Adult Arcade. There was nothing subtle about the Over 21 Bookstore.

The entrance to the "world famous" Over 21 Bookstore, photo courtesy of John O.

"The front was painted with all those caution yellow signs and flashing bulbs," recalled David Plomin. "Adult videos. Novelties. And painted on the façade of the building was, 'Come in and meet a friend.' I remember that."

"It was touted as the busiest adult bookstore," said Race Bannon. "That was on their advertisements. We would get people at the Glory Hole who came to see the world-famous Over 21 Bookstore next door. There was great synergy between the two. Guys would be at the bar and say, 'I'm going to go next door to get my dick sucked.' When they came back, they were usually wearing a smile. I went there quite a bit to talk with a friend of mine who worked at the front desk. I would just sit and watch all the men come and go."

A *Gay Life* newspaper ad for the Over 21 read, "Mention *Gay Life* and get $5 off any videotape in stock. The videotape headquarters! Chicago's largest array of visual entertainment. Video Tape. Film. X-rated erotica as never before. Magazines. Books. Rubber, Leather, and all your needs whatever the need. We are the ultimate adult shoppe. Open 24 hours every day!"

Being open around the clock seven days a week, the Over 21 was frequently looking for help. The bookstore's standard classified read, "Clerk Wanted—Positions available in Chicago's Number 1 adult bookstore. Must be neat in appearance. All hours open. Apply in person at 1347 N. Wells."

Since opening in 1971, the Over 21 Bookstore remained open all day every day until June of 1977, when the business was closed briefly for several operating violations. As reported by the *Chicago Tribune*, "Among the 20 violations alleged by building inspectors, [bookstore owner, Kenneth] Cameron said, there were complaints that the sex films are flammable, there is no 'natural' daylight in the windowless bookstore, and a wall isn't rat proof. 'This is a crock of b.s.,' Cameron said.

"Other complaints included allegations of unsafe electrical sockets and inadequate fire exits. ...Five patrons watching adult peep shows in the rear of the one-story building left within seconds after the plainclothes detectives entered the store, according to cashier Donald Terzwell.

"At least 15 other persons, several of them dressed in expensive suits, entered the store from outside but quickly withdrew ..." (Richard Phillips, 'City inspectors shut Old Town porn shop.' *Chicago Tribune,* June 11, 1977).

The bookstore crackdown came two weeks after acting Mayor Michael A Bilandic (1933-2002) aired his "porn war" platform. Bilandic assumed the office after Mayor Richard J Daley collapsed and died at his doctor's office on December 20, 1976.

Following several previous adult bookstore raids, a reporter asked Blandic if what he was doing was harassment. He replied, "Yes it is. They have been harassing the innocent people of the city, and we're not going to tolerate it." Bilandic went on to call adult bookstore operators "merchants of filth." (Davis, 'Bilandic defends porn war.' *Chicago Tribune*, May 27, 1977).

"At the Over 21 Bookstore the clerk was on a platform above the sales floor so he could look out over the shop, kind of keep an eye on things," recalled David Plambeck. "The Over 21 sold the usual stuff as I recall—toys, magazines, poppers, and dirty books."

"I remember coming to Old Town with five or six friends when I was in high school," said Richard F. "I think I had a fake ID that said I was 18. We went to the adult bookstore along there. The girls in the group were too embarrassed to go in, but my buddy and I did. We went back to where the booths were. He ducked in one and I ducked in another, only mine was marked gay. I was watching my first gay porno in there, and I was so excited and worried that when I came out of the booth, I would get busted by my buddy, which was what happened. But I just said, 'Wow, you wouldn't believe the size of that guy's dick.' North Wells was a big part of my sexual awakening."

For guys like Brian D Smith, the video porn store and arcade was little more than a means to an end. "I know I went there to suck cock or have my cock sucked, but nothing about it was too memorable. Those places were all over."

"That place was always busy, day and night," recalled Mercury. "I worked the front desk, and we sold a lot of products there—movies, magazines, toys, poppers, everything. We didn't make commission, but the owners were good about surprise bonuses. At the end of the shift, they might say, 'We did great today,' and give me an extra $100. They had two pit bulls for security. After I was hired, the first thing I did was meet the dogs. Working there was nice because it was one of the few adult bookstores where we didn't have to worry about what was going on in the back. Some places want you to tell people to keep feeding tokens in the machine, but not the Over 21."

Terence Alan Smith recalled, "I would be dancing at the Bistro, then go to the Over 21 and get a blow job, and then go back and dance some more."

Over 21 Bookstore advertisement, photo courtesy of Gay Life *newspaper.*

"I was never a fan of adult bookstores," said Carl R. "I had raid anxiety. I had been arrested in a raid years before. One night, I was too wound up to care. I went there and put down my money and was eager to get to the back. I ended up in a booth with this guy who asked to get fucked. So, I'm fucking him, and he is bent over with his hands on the bench. Suddenly, there was a loud knock on the door. The guy I'm fucking said, 'Don't worry, keep going.' So, I tried, but there was more banging on the door. So, I'm pulling up my pants, and my anxiety is very high. More banging on the door. When I opened it up, it was the guy from the front desk bringing me my change from admission."

"I picked up a guy at Carol's," said Phil Bernal. "He said he had a place to go. I thought we were going to his place, but we went to the Over 21 Bookstore. That was the place he had. We got together in a booth, but that was never my thing. I like more room, more space. I did not want a quickie in a booth."

Tigg hustled for a while along that stretch of Wells St. "Every time I tried to step foot inside the Over 21, they would tell me to get the fuck out. They thought I was too young. Chances are I was."

Malone Sizelove was met with an even less hospitable welcome. "Every time I walked into that place, the guy behind the counter pulled out this baseball bat and said, 'you are not allowed in here.' I have no idea if I reminded him of someone who had stolen from there or who had pissed in a booth or something."

"That place felt straight to me," recalled Daniel L. "I felt like I had to be cautious there, so I only went inside once or twice."

Robert Kimmons patronized the Over 21. "I didn't get it. I figured it was something more for straight guys. I didn't realize there was more beyond the front of the store. The first time I went through the turnstile of an adult bookstore and back into an arcade was at the Second Story Emporium (2827 N. Broadway)."

"I went to the Over 21 late at night to buy my gay skin rags," said Steve Lafreniere. "I remember you had to walk through the straight section to get to the rack with the gay magazines. There were a few magazines I bought regularly, so I know I was in there at least once a month to pick up those."

The 1982 *Drummer Magazine* piece on Chicago nightlife also covered the Over 21 Bookstore. "A long-time staple of the gay scene in Old Town, the Over 21 Bookstore remains one of the Windy City's most convenient and popular sites. The emphasis here is on selection, and the Over 21 has one of the Midwest's most diverse collections of gay erotica. Their offerings of toys ain't shabby either.

"And being conveniently located between the Glory Hole and Carol's Speakeasy, the traffic through the Over 21 can be eye-boggling."

In 1992, the *Chicago Tribune* reported that the Over 21 Bookstore had been the apparent target of a bomb. "The device had been placed in an alley behind the back door of the adult bookstore," stated the article. A man walking down the alley spotted the bomb and informed authorities. He described the device as, "silver and about the size of a hand grenade...It was almost as if someone wanted it to be found." (Angela Bradbery, Ron Grossman, 'Bomb found in North Side alley.' *Chicago Tribune*, April 17, 1992).

One door south of the Over 21 Bookstore, at 1345 N. Wells, a new adult bookstore came on the scene in January 1979. The Peeping Tom was gay adult arcade positioned a good way back from the sidewalk on the rear portion of the lot. The building was basically a two-story shed with a door and a small rectangular window. The Peeping Tom was on the first floor and the owner, William "Red" Wemette, resided in the apartment upstairs. In contrast to the flashing bulb and caution yellow façade of the Over 21 Bookstore, the Peeping Tom had little to no exterior fanfare or signage. Set back from the sidewalk, it was an easy place to walk right by unless you knew it was there, but plenty of guys knew about the Peeping Tom.

Dean Ogren recalled a big difference between the two. "The Over 21 had more the straight folks, a much straighter crowd, and the Peeping Tom was Gay! Gay! Gay! The first time I went there was with a friend of mine. I had never been to an adult peep show place before. I asked what to do, and my friend said, 'Just have fun; you'll figure it out.' There were probably 15 booths in there with gay porn movies and glory holes. My friend was right; it didn't take me long to figure it out."

Eventually, Ogren worked at the Peeping Tom on and off for a couple of years. "I was living at home at the time. My shift was 10 p.m. to 3 a.m.

I told my parents I was working at an all-night diner. That explained the hours. They took quarters, not tokens. I remember because my job was to knock on the door and make sure that guys kept on feeding the machines. If the light above the door went out, the movie wasn't running. I would give them a second, then knock and say, "Quarters. Quarters." That's all I said my whole shift. I tried to be nice about it. If they gave me cash, I got quarters for them. I still was not very popular. I was interrupting sex to tell them to pay money."

At the Peeping Tom, an open doorway separated the front counter from the arcade area. Admission was two dollars with a minimum of two dollars in quarters. Most guys gave the clerk a five and took three in quarters. The front area held just enough porn, poppers, and toys to qualify as a retail space. At the Peeping Tom, the arcade was the moneymaker.

When Diana McKay was becoming leatherman Daddy Dion, they would go to the Peeping Tom. "It was very sleazy, but that was one reason I went there. I remember the sticky floor. It was very dark. Another reason I went there was that I didn't want people to recognize me as Diana, and that place was too dark to see much of anything. There wasn't much of a front area. After paying you went straight back to the booth area."

David Plambeck went there a few times. "The booths were to the left as you walked inside. I recall it only being open at night, so I went to the Over 21 Bookstore much more."

"A couple times I met guys in the Glory Hole," said Mike F. "And they asked me if I wanted to go next door? The Peeping Tom was where we went. The back area was maybe a little bigger than the size of someone's garage, but it was quite active."

Rail remembers it being busy on weekends. "I hooked up there a lot and never had to worry about talking to those people again. A lot of the guys there, at least when I went, seemed to be on the down low. I liked it because I could go to Carol's and dance, go there and have sex."

"The Peeping Tom was called an adult bookstore, but I don't think there were any books in there," added Ogren. "It was really just a sex shop. The owner, who everyone said was a mobster, was this Irish ruffian-looking guy named Red. I only saw him once, but he scared me.

Frightening—like a mean-looking guy just out of prison. He made me afraid not to do a good job."

Roger Hickey stated in 1995, "Red was a real strange character. Everybody knew he carried a gun. Everybody knew that he was afraid of crowds and everything, so he would never go out. He would keep a very low profile. He was a person nobody trusted very much.

"…Then one day, we came into Carol's, and it seems that very early in the morning, the moving truck was there, moving all his stuff out of the apartment. Later in the day, there was another van that moved all the inventory out of the Peeping Tom. … And I guess they had blocked off part of the street and took Red out of the house in unmarked cars and put him in the Witness Protection Program, and he was never seen again. He apparently had video cameras in his apartment, over the bookstore and had all this great stuff on tape, which we subsequently saw on local newscasts when it all went to trial." (Jack Rinella Interviews, 1995).

According to federal authorities, Schweihs, aka 'the German,' was a top crime syndicate assassin. The affidavit stated that Schweihs had been taped 'while dropping strong hints' that he was involved in the shooting deaths of former Bijou operator Paul Gorsky as well as Patsy Riccardi, owner of the Admiral Theater.

"In the spring of 1987, Wemette allowed agents to install tape recording equipment in his apartment above the Peeping Tom. They taped 17 times over a 15-month period ending Aug. 7. "Throughout their secretly taped conversations, Schweihs made clear that he killed people for a living. In talking about moving in on Toushin, he mentioned that Toushin's former partner, Gonsky, 'had the accident outside my shed.'

"Gonsky was shot to death in 1976 in a parking lot at 1317 N. Wells St. At the time, Schweihs lived next door to the lot."

"Schweihs also spoke of Riccardi, former owner of the Admiral Theater, whose body was found in a trunk in 1985.

"Schweihs is quoted as telling Wemette that he picked up Riccardi at a motel near where Riccardi was last seen alive and had taken him for a ride in a 'smoker,' a mob term for a stolen car." (Kozol/O'Brien, 'Tapes detail life inside mob's porn world.' *Chicago Tribune*, Sept. 19, 1988).

Weeks later, the *Tribune* reported, "Two suspected crime figures, Frank J. Schweihs and Anthony Daddino were indicted for extorting $18,700 from the owner of the Peeping Tom (William Wemette) and his associate (Leonard Cross) through the "wrong use of violence and fear." In addition, the follow-up *Chicago Tribune* piece states, "Schwiehs was also indicted on charges that he attempted to extort 'a substantial sum of money' from Steven Toushin, owner of the Bijou Theater, 1349 N. Wells St." ('US jury indicts 2 on extortion charges.' *Chicago Tribune*, Oct. 14, 1988).

Schweihs died in 2008 at age 76. Daddino passed away the same year.

The Peeping Tom never reopened.

The "world famous" Over 21 Bookstore lasted a few more years, eventually closing with the rapidly changing streetscape of North Wells Street.

Gay Chicago

It was 1976, the country was in the middle of bicentennial fever, Jimmy and Rosalyn Carter were settling in at the White House. Bruce Jenner and Dorothy Hamill were the big winners at the Olympics, and everyone was ga-ga over the Hamill 'wedge.' *Rocky* (the first, though we didn't know it yet) won the Oscar for best picture, and *Gay Chicago* was born," wrote Rick Karlin on the 15th anniversary of the paper.

"Surviving 15 years in the publishing business is no easy feat. And, as one of the first publications that had the pride to use the 'G' word in our title (and still one of the few) we've faced our share of crises.... Through the years we've seen our ups and downs, but *Gay Chicago* has persevered and, in fact, has become the leading guide to entertainment in the gay and lesbian community." (Karlin, 'After Dark: Memories.' *Gay Chicago*, April 4, 1991).

A native of the North Side, *Gay Chicago* publisher, Ralph Paul Gernhardt (1934-2006) returned to the city in the early 1970s to teach radio broadcasting. In 1972, he started a telephone hotline with a recorded message that talked about gay bar events around town. The popularity of the phone line prompted Gernhardt to start *Gay Chicago* in 1976. Twenty years later, Gernhardt discussed his inspiration. "... I felt there was a need for something. At that particular time, the gay community didn't have any regular periodicals supplying information about what was going on in the community."

Gay Chicago, "the gay weekly for nightlife news," began publication in Gernhardt's apartment on the 1400 block of Wells St. When the first issue of the paper was published in Nov. 1976, it was a biweekly called *Gay News*. By 1977, the paper had become a weekly and the name was changed to *Gay Chicago News* for a few months before becoming *Gay Chicago*.

Lifelong newsman Dan DiLeo and publisher Ralph Paul Gernhardt, courtesy of Gay Chicago.

When *Gay Chicago* first began publication, as *Gay News*, it was put together in the second-floor apartment of publisher Ralph Paul Gernhardt at 1447 N. Wells St. "The art table was in the dining room," explained typesetter Karen Ross. "The offices were in one of the bedrooms. I had my desk with my electric typewriter. Ralph lived there with his partner, Michael. It was not unusual in the mornings to encounter tricks they picked up the night before at the Glory Hole."

In his memoir, Rick Karlin writes, "I got off the bus and walked two blocks over to the magazine's office on Wells Street. The address was for a storefront with apartments above. I double-checked the address, thinking I made a mistake, but it was correct. Then I discovered a side door and a bell listing Gernhardt Publications. I rang it, and when the buzzer sounded, I opened the door and walked up a steep flight of stairs.

"I opened the door and saw the spaces intended to serve as the living and dining rooms of the apartment filled with desks, all shrouded under a cloud of cigarette smoke..." (Karlin, *Paper Cuts My Life in Chicago's Volatile LGBTQ Press.* Rattling Good Yarns Press, 2019).

"When you showed up for work, you never knew what you were going to walk into," explained Erin Criss. "Drunken fights, half-naked guys— Ralph Paul and Michael fought like cats and dogs and the *Gay Chicago* office was right in the middle of it. And in the middle of all that was Dan DiLeo who was always chipper and happy."

Karen Ross added. "At *Gay Chicago*, every evening at 5 p.m., Dan DiLeo opened himself a beer. I don't like beer, so I declined. Dan asked what I drank, and I said scotch and water. So, he went out and bought a bottle of JB Scotch and every day from then on at 5 p.m., Dan would deliver a scotch and water to my desk. That 5 p.m. cocktail was a *Gay Chicago* ritual."

In his obituary for Dan DiLeo (1938-1989), Jon-Henri Damski wrote of the lifelong newsman, "Dan DiLeo and I, as beginners in mainstream journalism, had the same assignment, writing obituaries. Dan went on to be a typesetter, copy editor, rewriter, reporter, top investigative reporter, editorial writer, newspaper guild leader, and spokesperson. He brought all these skills to *Gay Chicago News* in 1977 and formed a lifelong partnership with Ralph Paul Gernhardt. Together, they became the co-publishers of *Gay Chicago Magazine*." DiLeo died of AIDS in 1989 at age 51.

"Ralph did not want a straight woman working there," said Erin Criss. "When I started working for the paper, Karen did the typesetting, and Michael K took photos. That was how I started. I took photos, and eventually, Ralph let me sell ads. He didn't want me to do that either. I tried explaining that the advertising market was bigger than he thought. I was proven right. My first sale was for a full-page ad from a designer children's store. When I approached the owner she said, 'I would love to reach that community with advertising.' After I came in with that check for a full-page ad, Ralph said, 'Okay, you can have the job.' ...When I was there, the Bijou spent a lot of money advertising in *Gay Chicago*. Ralph told me the Bijou was a big reason that *Gay Chicago* managed to stay in business in the early years."

Eventually, the operations of *Gay Chicago* moved from the confines of Ralph Paul's apartment to a storefront space a couple of doors down at 1437 N. Wells St.—the building that formerly housed the gay bar the Butterfly aka the Iron Butterfly.

Rick Karlin described the setup of the space after *Gay Chicago* moved in. "You walked into the *Gay Chicago* building vestibule; we were on one side. There was a newsstand across the hall that sold candy and cigarettes, magazines and newspapers, that kind of place. And straight back was an art gallery run by Andy Antoncyzk (1949-2022)." One key showing at Antoncyzk's gallery featured the work of Bob Fischer—the artist dubbed "the Windy City Warhol" by *People Magazine*.

Karen Ross loved working at the paper. She especially enjoyed managing the message board. Items for the message board could be dropped off at the paper or mailed to the *Gay Chicago* office. Ross added that there was a third option. "People would also bring me items for the message board to Sunday's (430 N. Clark), the gay dance bar where I worked as a cocktail waitress and bartender. People gave me messages for the paper to publish, sometimes on slips of paper and sometimes on cocktail napkins."

At the time, what is now called the River North area was a hive of gay nightlife. Within a few blocks of Sunday's were the Bistro, the Baton, the Gold Coast, the Redoubt, the Ritz, a couple of bathhouses, and more— making Sunday's a convenient drop off spot for message board bits. If you had trouble finding it, Sunday's had an upside down Old Style Beer sign above the entrance. The sign was a nod to the previous era when an upside down beer sign outside bars in parts of the Midwest was code that it was a gay bar or at least gay-friendly.

The original name of Sunday's was Sunday's Children and then it was shortened to Sunday's Child and eventually just Sunday's. The bar was named after the children's nursery rhyme. A copy of the *Monday's Child* poem was just inside the door. "Monday's child is fair of face, Tuesday's child is full of grace. Wednesday's child is full of woe, Thursday's child has far to go. Friday's child is loving and giving, Saturday's child works hard for a living. But the child that is born on Sabbath day is bonny and blithe, good and GAY!!"

Ross continued, "Most people had nicknames on the message board—mine were Blue Eyed Bitch and Ruby Red Lips. Messages were free and we would get up to 100 in an issue—flirtations, people being silly, being goofy back and forth. Back then everyone was very connected through bar culture. Everyone went out all the time. The message board was just another way for people to connect and have more fun."

Come Party With

Karen (The Message Girl)

On Her Birthday
Friday, Sept. 14th— 11 p.m.

SUNDAY'S
430 N. CLARK ST.

Karen Ross, the woman behind the Gay Chicago *message board, courtesy of the paper.*

The message board was often wildly inappropriate, sometimes timely and political, and thoroughly engrossing to read. It was a community gossip column for the nightlife crowd, a fascinating relic from a pre-chat-room world. As the artifact of a bygone era, the message board offers another perspective and point of entry into LGBT Chicago from almost 50 years ago. So imagine taking a seat on a bar stool, flipping open the latest issue of *Gay Chicago,* and squinting in the dim bar light to read:

—Last Weeks Toy. Careful ... he enjoys breaking his new toys and then discarding them into a crowded heap. The Marionette.

—Scott, now that your love life is on the rocks, why don't you come explore my rocks? Bobby.

—Leatherman Tex: Tallulah, whore to all Babylon, is intrigued by you whoever you are. I am currently single and looking for either a good lay or a good husband or both. If you sweat when you have sex, it could be a match made in Chicago.

—Samantha: Was curious to see the Steamworks you rave about. Almost missed the door, but I knew it had to be your place: The big sign Sam's Discount was above the door. Hanging out your shingle? Do you still give them (shingles) or is it S&M green now? Stamp Collector.

—Cornelius: I'd like to take you on a Friday night journey through Rogers Park and show you how cold it is. Night Watchman. P.S. You must be bored also!

—Sweet William, Sleaze is your middle name? I agree. It can't be mine though, the initials would be too tacky. Disco Al.

—Chicago, I'm on my way in for a weekend. Looking forward to seeing you soon. To Cliff, get your gown cleaned, bitch, we're going out. To Dick, see you at the Hole? To Karen, see you at Sundays? ... Oh, and one more thing. Renee of Wells St. do you remember those nights we snuck under the gate to the Glory Hole's pool to...? I do. Danny (Houston)

—Elmer, I don't want to pussy foot around. Let's get high on catnip and bite feet.

—Aunt Daleen, I hear you're "redecorating" your apartment again and again and again. Is it true there's a special on duck blinds?

—Phil-lips (of Hawthorne Mellody). When am I going to be introduced to your needle dick in-law? Were there a lot of hot rocks in the Smokies? I bet there were, you bitch!! Love and kisses, Uncle Dick.

P.S. For nothing could be sweeter than my peter in your seater (that's a warning).

—Bucky Beaver loves Chipmunk Cheeks!

—Nickel, Next time you throw a glass of wine make sure it's a good year. Love you, Renee of Wells Street

Gay Chicago's Bulletin Board

★ MESSAGES ★

Mrs. Ex: Cluck, cluck you crazy woman, U.S.S. Cover Boy

George & Jackie: Just in case you didn't know, Mom was the only one who went to Germany. The rest of your "family" is still here and concerned. Love ya, Jeff

Danny: V-V-V-V-R-R-R-R-O-O-O-M-M-M!!! Me

Karen: Let's all get fucked up. Let's keep a good thing going. Love, Your Son, Billy

The Two "Go-Go" Dancers at the Speakeasy are wasting their talents there. They are out of sight. An Admirer

Thank you for your support and donations:
Big Red's: Beer, Ice & Storage
Gold Coast, Beer
Frog Pond, Beer, Wine
Flight, Beer, Ice, Every Week
Sunday's, Beer
Cheeks, Beer, Schnapps
State Street Deli, Food Provisions
Ultra Ink, Inc., Transportation
G.A.A., Board of Directors

Herb: You were superb. Keep the lucky hat on and keep snapping back. A Friend

Chuck: Let's invite more straight people to our bars. It's one way of ending the sex which belongs at home anyways.

RRs J & ?: I know a skilled surgeon with years of experience at separating Siamese Twins. Unless I get to walk ahead of you, tossing chain links at the ceremony, I'll give him your names. Red Rider

Bordello Rose: Tell us, what exciting, adventurous tour/outing are you going to cancel next? Midwest Valiums

J.J.: Boom, boom, boom. Kick those legs, strut your stuff, dance, dance, dance. you dizzy Queen. Pinball Fred

★ MESSAGES ★

Diane: Thank you for never doubting me, and for your trust in me. Let's go zooming again soon. Jeff

Allen: I'll call one of these days. I mean it. Kevin (Sunday's)

Ssttilcckk litt, Sshhaaddoooww!! Porka

Tinkerbelle: Don't play with your ball and jacks in the Clark, try to be a lady. Ha! Ha! Father

A.J.: When are we going skating together? Love ya, Spike

No. 310: 18 E.E. just won't be the same anymore. No. 710

Dear Michael:
HAPPY BIRTHDAY
Love, Karen

Little George: Great, wonderful, marvelous and simply fantastic to see you again after a long, long time. You look great! And you're a real sweetheart. Don't make it so long next time. Love, Karen

DDT: Next barbeque, no chicken, just the landlord. Love ya all. Spike

Dora: You are so so so so sweet to me!!! Doodle

Thanks Sunday's and Flight: You're good neighbors. Love, The Ranch (Sam/Tom & Staff)

B.J.: With the whole city after you, I hardly

The Gay Chicago *message board, courtesy of the paper.*

—Continue your boycott of Florida citrus products. Anita has signed another one-year contract and we continue to be oppressed.

—To Mike: Now you can freshen your cologne in between those songs with the high notes. I'll watch the door while you're gone and when you return you can practice spiking the ball. P.U.

—Michael & George: Welcome to Chicago. Sure nice to have you here.

—B.J. Warren: What's all this fan mail about? I don't think you're so HOT! After all, take away your good bod, groovy hair length, dimples, inviting eyes, mustache, laugh lines under your eyes ... oh well, I guess I may as well join them rather than fight them!

—To the short, cute, desk day clerk at Man's Country: Belated thanks for loaning me 50 cents for bus fare one afternoon. Appreciative.

—Gregg (of Over 21 Bookstore): Belated Happy Birthday. Now that we know that you are over 18 (x 1.7). Midwest Valiums.

—DDT: Next barbeque, no chicken, just the landlord. Love ya all. Spike

—Glory Hole: Congratulations on finally getting your 4 a.m. license back—now I must ask my boss for a raise to pay for two more hours of pinball. I hope that you don't lose and get it all back again as I couldn't stand another glass of that horrible champagne. Pinball Fred.

—Morticia: I hear you're back in the streets again! Don't say MAN-HOLE cover to me, dear! Gutter Patrol

—A.J.: Found any hot cab drivers lately? Guess Who?

—Betty Boop: How many bands of gold will this make or did you lose count? Mark

—To the one on the patio in the brown suit at 431 W. Roscoe. You look good through binoculars. Cute ass. Can I taste it?

—Maurice: A love so wrong turned out to be so right, let's keep it and never get silly again. Happy 6 months to us. Me.

Ross added, "Before AIDS, the first thing people would open to in the paper was the astrology page and then they would go to the message board. After AIDS, people opened the paper and went right to the obituaries." As the epidemic descended upon the community, *Gay Chicago* provided up-to-the-moment information about AIDS/HIV, safer sex, and various local AIDS agencies. In addition to medical reportage, the paper touched upon every aspect of the disease—financial planning, health and wellness tips, insurance advice, political commentary, etc.

The paper also continued to be a leading source for LGBT nightlife and doings, top gay sports coverage, editorials, classifieds, photos, gossip, interviews, and a roster of popular columnists. The paper was growing quickly and *Gay Chicago* soon outgrew the 1437 N. Wells Street space.

In his memoir, *Paper Cuts,* Rick Karlin writes, "...additional advertisers meant extra ad salespeople, and they needed space for desks. It was time to move again. Ralph and Dan found office space on the second floor of a parking garage on Broadway, south of Belmont." (Karlin. *Paper Cuts My Life in Chicago's Volatile LGBTQ Press*. Rattling Good Yarns Press 2019).

Karen Ross recalled when the paper moved from the North Wells Street building to the larger offices at 3115 N. Broadway. "They were moving desks and boxes, moving more all around me until I was the only one left in the old office. All the furniture and cabinets and everything were gone. It was just me working at the typesetting machine. The issue had to get done. I was the last to leave. I was typing until the minute the old location of *Gay Chicago* was locked and closed."

Epilogue

Looking Back From the End of the Block

Educator Steve Migalski takes his students on a walking queer tour of Wells Street every year. "That Wells Street stretch is such pure evidence of queer erasure. Old Town was once very queer, but it's not queer now. It used to feel special. North Wells was the center of the youth movement and the counterculture movement and then a center of queerness and all that feels gone."

Malone Sizelove shared, "For a while, that stretch of Wells Street was our Times Square. Seeing that stretch, I feel that pain of nostalgia. I'm not generally a nostalgic guy but driving down that street and seeing it now is sad. There is nothing left to remind you of what it was."

Form for the coloring contest put on by the Glory Hole in honor of the Old Town Art Festival, courtesy of Gay Chicago.

Acknowledgments

When I was looking for a publisher, I could not have landed at a better place than Rattling Good Yarns Press. Once again, huge thanks to Ian and Sukie for their guidance and care.

Allen Patrykus, thank you for being so generous with your time, your memories, and your photographs. Your input filled in so much of the story.

Thanks to Chicago's two excellent LGBTQ community resources — the Gerber Hart Library and Archives, as well as the Leather Archives and Museum.

As always, thanks to all the journalists, photographers, newspapers, and magazines that have helped to document Chicago LGBTQ history.

This book would have been impossible without the dozens of folks who shared their memories about the 1300 block of North Wells. Thanks to all of you. Your memories helped to capture the block and give the book its soul.

About the Author

Queer historian and writer Owen Keehnen is the author of several fiction and nonfiction titles. He has penned several books on LGBTQ Chicago, including *Dugan's Bistro and The Legend of the Bearded Lady* and *Man's Country: More Than a Bathhouse*. He coauthored, with Tracy Baim, biographies on three Chicago gay community legends: Chuck Renslow, Jim Flint, and Vernita Gray. Keehnen worked with St Sukie de la Croix on three installments of the *Tell Me About It* book series. His next book from Rattling Good Yarns Press will be *A Place for Us, Gay Life at Chicago's Belmont Rocks*. He is the co-founder of the LGBTQ history and education organization, the Legacy Project. Keehnen was inducted into the Chicago LGBT Hall of Fame in 2011. He lives in the Rogers Park neighborhood of Chicago with his husband, Carl, and his dogs, Vince and Daisy.